In the Quest

of

Paradise

by

Ingrid Heller

Based on a true story

Order this book online at www.trafford.com
or email orders@trafford.com

Most Trafford titles are also available at major online book retailers.

Printed in the United States of America.

ISBN: 978-1-4269-4705-6 (sc)
ISBN: 978-1-4269-4706-3 (e)

*Our mission is to efficiently provide the world's finest, most comprehensive book publishing
service, enabling every author to experience success. To find out how to publish your
book, your way, and have it available worldwide, visit us online at www.trafford.com*

Trafford rev. 11/02/2010

 www.trafford.com

North America & international
toll-free: 1 888 232 4444 (USA & Canada)
phone: 250 383 6864 ♦ fax: 812 355 4082

THE TABLE OF CONTENTS

CREATION
The First Six Days 3
The Seventh Day 13

THE DIVINE COMEDY
Popes 27
Concepcion 41
Hope 45
Records 51
Virgo 59
Promise 65
Adam and Eve 71
Prayer of the Virgin 75
Good News 79
Answered Prayer 87
Antwerpen 91
Alchemist 95
Heron 103
From Louvre to Lourdes 109
Magic Flute 117
Hermes 121
Mystical Marriage 127
Archon 131
Pelican 137
Guides 141

Gnosis	149
A'dam	151
The Divine Comedy by Dante	155
Canto XXV	161
Toledo	167
From Alberto to Alberta	173
Ariel	179
Pamela	185
Eden	189
Lamen	193
Canto XXVI	199
Death and the Maiden	203
Alchemy	207
Messages	211
Pentagram	219
Closure	223
Santiago	225
Coincidences	229
Priorities	239
Reflection	245
About the Author	249

**This book is a revised edition of the
Divine Comedy by Beatrice**

Dedicated to my children, friends, relatives and everyone I am to meet.

Especially dedicated to those who work tirelessly in bridging our reality with the higher one, on behalf of the Creator and the Creation.
Thanks to their service, Humanity and Earth are ascending, according to the Divine Plan of the eons ago. Our contribution of Unconditional Love vibration is all that is asked of us to assist and participate in the Creation of true Paradise on Earth.

CREATION

THE FIRST SIX DAYS

HONEYMOONS initiate new beginnings, and sometimes the end. On our honeymoon in Europe, my husband insisted that I must visit Chile. It was a country where I lived for thirty months with my ex-husband and my children, making many friends in the countryside where we lived. They were dear to me. Verne hoped that my visit would liberate me from the worry I had about my friends' well-being and give me a chance to clear the past, as he put it. I chose summer vacation for the trip, when I could be replaced by my daughter Monica, who was eighteen then and would look after her four younger siblings. My decision to travel to Chile was accompanied by anxiety close to fear of death. It was a very uncomfortable feeling I didn't remember having ever, and I had no idea how to interpret it. It was so strong on some days that I decided to subjugate it and find out what was ahead of me, regardless.

The trip started with coincidences and ended with coincidences. While waiting at the Toronto airport for the boarding call for our flight to Buenos Aires, I was occasionally checked out by a half sleeping passenger, a gentleman in his early sixties with a very handsome elongated face. When I got to my seat on the plane, he happened to be sitting right across the aisle. It turned out that his Japanese neighbour could speak only his language and I too was seated next to Japanese travellers. I asked the flight attendant if we could swap our seats. She consented. The handsome man was thrilled and said that his first wish came true. He was Spanish and Italian speaking, flying to Buenos Aires where he lived. I was English and Spanish speaking, flying to Santiago de Chile. It was a ten-hour flight. He had already flown from Rome and spent a couple of days in Toronto. He wanted to see Canada, he said. During a vigorous turbulence over Puerto Rico, he said his second wish was coming true. I asked what that was and he said that he would like to end up with me alone on a small island. It was clear to me after more delicious comments were directed toward my person that I was his fantasy, which probably began in Toronto. I was "the Divine Woman, the one that captured the imagination of poets", he said. I enjoyed his reverent gaze and to his delight I let him share my pillow for a while. Otherwise, he was a proper gentleman and made my flight very enjoyable.

On my arrival in Santiago, I was welcomed by a clear view of the Andes. Rain grounds the city's pollution for a few hours until it all ends up in smog and hell again. No one was informed about my arrival. For a couple of years, none of my letters sent to ex-neighbours families were answered. I began to suspect something unusual. While on the bus to Rancagua, I observed the many changes along the highway. Chile's economy was strong by then, well-governed and trouble-free. I got off at the exit to Graneros and slowly walked toward the town, pulling my large suitcase behind. Shortly after, I was picked up by a cab driver, who took me to *"quarta hijuela"*, our former rural road. The driver stopped in front of neighbour's prefabricated house. Señora Rosa stepped out of door to see who had arrived. Surprised and in tears, she rushed over to hug me and asked right away if we were coming back. I told her that I was divorced from Eduardo and re-married to a Canadian man. She wondered why I didn't let them know. Clearly, our correspondence was blocked. Neither their letters they kept on sending us had arrived. Sheba just passed away, I was told. The beautiful German shepherd, that seemed to take to me instantly, was her daughter. This took care of one of my concerns. Sheba was our dear pet and we had to leave her behind when we left Chile. I couldn't imagine doing that to her again. I was offered to use one of three bedrooms in the house. It used to be a bedroom of our friends Nano and Orietta, whose lives ended in tragedy. I was warned that the bed moved sometimes, as if someone tried to get the occupant off. When that happened on the first night, I sent Nano to the Light. Anxiously, I was listening to hear about everyone, finding out that Marcela, the younger daughter of Rosa and Pilo had become a schoolteacher in town and that Patricia was married. Everyone from the community did relatively well. Our former house was occupied by the vineyard administrator at this time. Rosa's husband Pilo arrived from work in the evening. He worked in a meat plant in Rancagua at this time. Was he ever happy to see me! Patricia was to visit the next day, I was told. She lived in the neighbouring region with her husband, who trained horses there for income.

I waited for Patricia, who had become a pretty woman in her twenties. She was all excited telling me about her life. Later on, we headed toward our former *parcela*. It was a clear day with crisp wind blowing from the south. I was quiet and focused, selecting each step carefully to avoid puddles on the clayish country road. Now, I walked toward a piece of land I worked, toward a house we built, toward a place we left two years later, in the middle of Chilean winter as moist and unpredictable as it was those six years ago when we moved to this location for good. At this moment I felt like a defeated warrior, or a dreamer, not knowing what the next moment would bring, just as it felt those few years ago. Nobody could understand why I had chosen this country to settle in, why I left the comfort of Canadian city life, with a beautiful house, a garden and safe places for children's play, a school around the corner; all wonderful securities my life offered. Instead of giving myself some time after a divorce, I jumped into another marriage. Of course, I had all kinds of reasons that my friends learned to accept eventually, yet, when I was leaving Canada with my Chilean hubby, the three children from the previous marriage, three pet German shepherd dogs and ten suitcases, I was sure my friends questioned the state of my mind.

"Why don't you go to visit first, check it out? Why do you burn all bridges?" they suggested a number of times.

How could they understand the power of commitment to a change? It is like a new lifetime! It has to be one hundred percent! Even before I met Eduardo, I felt a magnetic pull toward South America, toward west coast, somewhere, where the sword shaped country was. Despite some obstacles, we moved. In reality, I had no idea what the real cause was or what the future was to bring. I lived every moment of each time, again, and all over again.

Patricia was a quiet companion. By now, I knew everything about her husband, her pregnancy and their plans for an immediate future.

The first days of my visit were reserved for people of this small town and community. My children and I had fond memories of them, sharing their fate. They touched our lives deeply and our souls remained connected to theirs into eternity.

"Señora Ingrid, did you notice a clear view of Cordillera?" Patricia reminded me.

Lost in my thoughts, I stopped for a moment, gazing at the surroundings and not too distant Cordillera de Los Andes. More memories began to pour in, like the inundating river that damaged so much in the country in the winter of 1982. What a year it was!

"I always enjoyed the view here, the fresh air, and the comforting sound of crickets, frogs and birds. Patricia, I loved it here, but, to stay here became impractical. I couldn't get out of this mud to give birth to Maria in the hospital on most of the days near my labour. I couldn't go through something like that again! Andrew had to be born in Canada! It was much harder to leave Chile than Canada. We planned on coming back..... I had not completed my journey here. Just don't ask me what it is; I don't know myself, Patricia."

We resumed the walk, until Patricia stopped again.

"Can you recognize it, Señora Ingrid?"

I looked ahead in disbelief.

"What happened to the trees, the orchard we've planted? Patricia, they cut down the trees along the canal! It looks so bare now! Why has someone cut them down? They were so beautiful!"

"Señora, the new owner needed to plant grape vines. He left your old house and lived in your big one. He spoke proudly of the good job you've done on it."

I heard Patricia's voice from a distance, its volume fading away. I stood next to the guardian of the entrance, by the old willow tree, caressed by her long thin branches. Staring into nothingness, I heard voices of my children and barking of dogs. I felt my fingers dipping into the soil, planting, weeding, bleeding. Against the mountain horizon, the hand-washed laundry was flapping dried in the wind on the clothes line. The baby Maria was resting in the basket under this weeping willow....'Someone is stealing your corn!' called out the neighbour....'They're not sincere with you, Señora!' warned another. 'Why don't your relatives help you more, Señora?' asked everyone.... Another chicken died, another puppy.... Rats are eating the food supply.... The last batch of flour was used up for bread making; the last portion of yeast.....a neighbour sends ox tails for broth....; 'How long will it take to make a soup, Mommy?'...'Sorry, children, we must give it to dogs this time; they haven't eaten for three days.'...' Mom, Baron died this morning!'.... 'What? I gave him water last night! Where is he?' ... 'By the dog house, Mom.'.... First grave by the lily garden....Another night with little sleep... Another UFO. Why are they here? ....So much blood running down my thighs. Oh, God, this child must live! They were so kind in the hospital - no charges....

I embraced the willow tree, reaching to security of the present moment. "Oh, my faithful friend, you know it all!"

"Are you all right, Señora Ingrid? You're crying and talking to the tree!"

"Patricia, this tree knows the whole story, yet, it cannot speak. It talked to my baby Maria. It witnessed the baptism of my four children. This tree somehow kept on saying to me that I had to be in this country. I wish I knew why."

"Our city women wouldn't put up with what you had taken on. I am sure there is something very special for you here.... Do you want to walk back now?"

I took a short moment yet to look back at our former home. I was aware that I'd be back and maybe at some other time visiting with my children and the husband. Ready to part with the past, I reached into my winter jacket pocket for the camera to take a few pictures. This act helped me over a threshold, giving me a distance of time. I became a tourist.

Three days later, July 12, 1988

It was easy to persuade Patricia to come with me to Santiago. I had planned to visit Mendoza in Argentina to treat myself to view the landscape of Cordillera de Los Andes on the way, taking a bus. The family insisted that I must travel accompanied. Patricia planned on asking her uncle, a policeman by profession, to travel with me. His niece was one of former exiles, operating a modest guest house in Mendoza. The uncle visited her frequently, always helping with an up-grade of premises.

Upon arrivals to Santiago, I reserved a room in the downtown hotel Libertador on the main avenue commonly called Alameda. Its real name is Bernardo O'Higgins, after the liberator of Chile from Spain who established an independent state in early eighteen hundreds. Our room was comfortable, but shortly after we settled in, something in the air triggered a cough that persisted for most of the evening. The students of the two universities on Alameda organized a demonstration against the present Junta government and we had been exposed through our room windows to the tear gas used to disperse the crowd.

To my surprise, Patricia welcomed the aftermath cleansing. She laughed when commenting on her constipation caused by pregnancy and that it took a bomb to relieve it. We also talked about more serious subjects - democracy was one of them.

"Chileans want democracy, Señora. Students are the voice of people."

"Do you think that Chileans are ready for democracy?"

"What do you mean, Señora Ingrid?"

"You see, Patricia, with democracy there is responsibility. It is time consuming to keep up with all information, to elect the right party, the right leader. Are Chileans ready?"

"I never thought about it that way. We are tired of the military regime! We want a change!"

"The militaries kept the country out of trouble from the outside. But, they couldn't protect you from the inside power - the Church." I deliberately accentuated the last word.

"I can't believe you are saying these words, Señora!" Patricia was evidently upset. "I always thought that you were a spiritual woman!"

"You said it, Patricia. Spiritual, but not religious, though I pray, I had my children baptized, I recognize the value of religious archetypes, and I have a relationship with the Creator. My spirituality is my personal inner journey, not a belief in dogma or doctrine the organized religion is projecting into human minds. Life itself is sacred, Patricia. A human being was given a free will and has a right to apply it and learn about consequences of the choice. Catholic Church is a powerful political party, in my opinion. And, it has got its foothold in South America!"

"The Cardinal is coming...."

"What?" I immediately responded with concern. "When is he coming?"

"This coming week. There will be an important meeting in Concepción."

"It sounds like a conception of some big changes. It is a crucial time, Patricia."

"Señora, is there something that you know and none of us know? I mean, in Canada you must hear all kinds of news!"

"I don't track what media is spreading, Patricia. When we stay away from any kind of mind programming, another network becomes available to our mind. I call it truth."

"How can you tell a difference between truth and deceit, Señora?"

"We feel it in our gut. Before believing anything, we must pay attention to our intuition. With some practice, we learn to tell a difference. There is a trap, though! The Ego steps between our thoughts. It teaches us as it misguides and confuses us; it becomes our enemy and a friend at the same time. Do you remember Jesus' saying 'Love your enemies'? We learn from our enemies much more than from our friends. We grow faster among opposition. Individuals, and countries alike, should go through this process."

Patricia was silent for a while, thinking about what I said.

"Señora, is any country ready for democracy? I mean, you live in a democratic country, you must know!"

"Dear Patricia, even in countries with long history of democracy, they become dysfunctional. Our representatives are just people with their own agendas."

"Many Chileans want the change, many don't. Chile was stable and prosperous in recent years. Do you think there is hope for our democracy?"

"Consciousness, Patricia, is the key to improvement. In the future, we will have enlightened leaders and citizens. Before that happens, we'll go through series of changes."

"The world is corrupt now, isn't it?"

"You got that right! Eventually, that will change. Every a newborn child brings a higher consciousness into our world. Individually, we can change things by positive attitude. We only have power to change ourselves from within, setting an example."

It was time to change a subject and talk about what is, rather than what could be.

"Are you happy in your marriage, Señora Ingrid?" asked Patricia's tired voice.

"Yes, I am. How about you, Patricia?"

"My husband is the first man I've ever had. I like being married. How did it feel for you when you got married the third time?"

"This wedding ceremony was special. The pastor who married us knew me. At first, he didn't want to wed us. He kept on saying that this man was not for me. Then Verne assured him that he wants to help me to raise my children, to be my partner for life and that he would support me in my endeavours. The pastor friend consented then."

"Your husband is very handsome. Is he good with your children?"

"Very good, Patricia. He also sent me on this trip. On our honeymoon in Europe, he gave me the trip after we visited Duomo in Florence. I will never forget that moment and the associated feelings ... we kept on looking at the fresco painting of Dante Alighieri by Domenico di Michelino, with images of Hell, Purgatory and Paradise, some Florentine buildings and a tall strong featured Dante in the center, with the crown of laurels on his head, dressed in red and holding a book - The Divine Comedy. We were somehow fascinated by Dante's face. He radiated wisdom, knowledge, commitment, love, devotion, and sadness. He was a man of exile, trying to enlighten people through his works. A great poet!"

"Tell me more about him!"

"I don't know much. His writings were inspired by love for Beatrice whom he saw while very young for the first time and then in company of her lady friend in their late teens. He never forgot her. She must have taken his breath away. He was an educator, writer, was involved in cultural, financial and political affairs of Florence and when his political party lost, he had to go into exile, wandering place to place, until he ended up in Ravenna, where he continued writing. His love for Beatrice was of pure and divine nature and she, as his complementary female, kept on guiding him throughout the writing of Paradiso of his Divine Comedy. This happened in early thirteen hundreds."

"Do you think that the painting inspired your husband to send you here?"

"I wondered about that, Patricia. He kept on repeating it since then, until I booked a flight. He actually said that he would like me to go to Chile as soon as possible."

"Did he give you any reason?"

"He said that I had some unfinished business here, some unresolved affairs and that it would be nice for me to get in touch with my friends from whom I wasn't getting any communication for some time. He knew I worried."

"Did you, Señora?"

"Naturally, Patricia! I wrote letters, sent them registered and, no word. Yes, I was concerned."

"Strange, isn't it? We've written too and never got any answer. At times we thought that you moved or that something had happened."

"Some things are unexplainable, Patricia."

Once more, I reviewed in my mind events of the last four years, drifting away with thoughts.

"Well, aren't you getting sleepy, Patricia?"

No answer. Patricia was asleep. I watched her for a while, thinking of the days when she had been making surprise visits to give me a hand with some housework. There was always so much to do! Patricia's help was treasured. Friendship grew despite the age difference. Now, she rested peacefully in a warm room, comfortable after a warm shower. A faithful companion she was.

THE SEVENTH DAY

Santiago, July 13th, 1988

I GOT UP early in the morning, trying to be as quiet as possible, not to awaken Patricia, who'd been up so many times during the night. First I checked the day timer. I had marked addresses of manufacturers I hoped to contact about possible exportation of their products to Canada. One office was right in downtown and other two in the industrial area of Santiago. Patricia's uncle offered to drive us places I wanted to visit.

I stepped into a bathroom to get ready. Concerned about the broken sleep at night, I glanced into the mirror to see how much puffiness there was left in my eyelids and under my eyes; what the darkness of the night has done to the whiteness of my complexion. My image indicated the contrary. There was no sign of the sleepless night! I looked to myself more beautiful than ever! Could my eyesight be affected by the smoke? I went back in the room. Patricia was up, sitting in her bed.

"Señora, you are looking so beautiful today!"

"Beautiful?"

"Yes, Señora! Radiant!"

13

"Let me see!" I stepped back into the bathroom, closing the door behind. I looked into the mirror again. Yes, my image was radiant! And there was a very vital feeling all over my body! I also noticed that my body was permeated with vibrancy and appeared more voluptuous, which was like that only during the first months of pregnancies. I had to acknowledge an exceptional beauty of form identifying with me. Could I be pregnant? According to my records, it was inconceivable. I let my gown fall on the tile floor beneath my feet, just to lay a silky mat to walk farther from the mirror, to observe more of feminine beauty. I lifted my arms and flexed them behind my long neck. The Goddess was back! Aphrodite and I could be twins! I wished I could stay like that forever. I almost defied gravity! From every angle the sight was more than pleasing. In regret, I took a deep breath. My husband was not there to enjoy and witness the multidimensional slender fullness, to give me pleasure of sharing the harvest of my fruit. A warm shower was a sad substitute for intimacy, but, after all, thousands of tiny fingers energizing and covering the epidermis garment of my body satisfied the longing.

The phone rang. Patricia was quick to pick it up. It was her uncle Manuel. He could not drive us anywhere on that day. Due to vehicular restriction to control pollution, drivers of cars with final digits of his licence plate number would be penalized. This changed the day's programme. We postponed the afternoon commitments for another day.

"This gives us some extra time in downtown, Patricia. We can do some smart shopping. I should call my husband at his work. I miss him!"

"Your husband should see you today, Señora. You always looked feminine and attractive, but today you look incredibly special."

"I appreciate your compliments, Patricia. I wish they came from my bride-groom's mouth!" I was grateful for Patricia's encouraging words. They confirmed what I saw and felt in my body – an incredible lightness of being since I woke up.

"Call your husband!"

I was lucky to get through the lines. Clearly, my husband didn't expect my call.

"Verne, how are you? I wish you were here, I miss you so much!"

There was no response.

"Verne? Are you there?"

"Yeah, I am listening," was his answer.

"How is everything? Are the children alright?"

"Everything is fine. We'll meet you at the airport next week. The same time of arrival?"

"Yes, darling. I love you! I miss you!"

No answer.

"Verne? Do you hear me?"

"Yes, I do. I cannot say too much here. People are listening."

"You cannot say to your wife that you love her? I don't believe this, Verne! They were at our wedding and you said it at the altar in front of everyone!"

There was no comment.

"Give my love to the children! I have to get some gifts for them yet. You still want the Argentine leather jacket, right?"

"Only if it is possible."

"Of course, it is. I am leaving for Mendoza in two days."

"Is it safe to go there, Ingrid? I hope I don't have to worry about you!"

"Absolutely safe! Patricia's cousin Roberto is coming with me and we are taking a bus together with his uncle, who is visiting a niece there. People are kind here."

"Enjoy the trip, dear!" were my husband's last words.

"Next time we'll travel together. Bye, love!"

I hung up and stared out the window for a while, not paying any attention to the walls of dark grey colour, neither to the asbestos roof of the lower neighbouring building. Even the sky was colourless.

"You look sad, Señora," said concerned Patricia.

"Sometimes, I don't understand my husband. His moods swing from one day to the other. I am disappointed! He was cold!"

"Men don't show their emotions easily, Señora."

"Remember, Patricia, when I told you about my fears prior to this trip?"

"I remember well. You were afraid that something might happen to you. You thought you would die!"

"Right! Verne actually tried to talk me out of the trip a day before the flight, 'Honey, if you feel that you might die, I don't want you to go. It is better to lose fifteen hundred dollars than you. Stay home and forget about the trip", I animated Verne's voice.

"Yes, Señora Ingrid, and you chose to find out what the fear was all about and went anyway."

"Right! So, here I am. Don't you think my husband should be a bit concerned?"

"I think he trusts you, Señora, and must know that you're brave and clever."

"Am I silly? I'm probably worrying about nothing. You're right, Patricia. He trusts me. Otherwise, he would not send me here. Before the wedding he was insecure and always jealous, without having a reason. He grew out of it. He does want me to enjoy this trip. I am going to do just that! Ready for breakfast?"

"Starving! There is nothing left in me; all is gone!"

We descended on foot to the lower dining room floor. It was a half-full. The waiter served us quickly. I was a bit intimidated by the attention we received and more so after Patricia commented,

"Señora, all the men are looking at you!"

"Is there something wrong with my hair?"

"They are looking at your radiance!"

"Oh, right! I forgot that I was radiant today. Maybe we should tell them that my husband doesn't give a damn, or that last night we kept on flushing the toilet."

"Cheer up, Señora. What will we do this afternoon?"

"I thought of going to the Canadian Embassy and give them my contacts, in case the children need to reach me. They might also recommend good manufacturers."

"Good idea! It is on this street just two blocks away. It would be my first time on Canadian territory!"

"We'll have a nice leisurely afternoon, Patricia. The day will be colourful despite the sky's greyness."

It didn't take much to make me feel enthusiastic. When I was a child, I preferred to laugh, play, dance and sing. Sadness brought only suffering and dark thoughts. I refused to dwell on nightmares and strongly disliked scary fairy tales. Why does anyone want to frighten little children? I always thought. Adults seemed so detached when I was growing up. When I finally left my native Bohemia twenty years ago, a new world opened up before my eyes. I fell in love with Canada. I learned that love for a country can be as strong as love for people. I knew about falling in love and being in love.

Downtown of Santiago is a very busy place, especially in the heart of city, where hotel Libertador is located. Patricia and I visited a sales office of company that was producing high quality woollen fabrics. Chile, just like Argentina and Brazil, excels in products made of leather. We checked the quality in the many shoe and accessories stores. I made some purchases and after the lunch we headed back in the direction of Calle Ahumada, where the Embassy was located. I kept very quiet, minding my own business. I learned a long time ago that an eye contact can provoke a reaction I may not desire. I intended to practise it very faithfully. Besides, the available space to get ahead was limited. At times, I had to break away from Patricia's arm to avoid a collision with another human being. I accelerated my pace to reach to our destination

"Slow down Señora! We are going in the wrong direction. The Embassy is over there!" Patricia pointed into the opposite direction than I had chosen.

"I know where I am going, Patricia. Just follow me," I answered calmly. I was not thinking about anything; I was content with the peace I felt within me.

Patricia looked puzzled, but assuming that I might be going somewhere else first, she kept on walking with me, arm in arm.

I stopped for a while, noticing a group of young people displaying banners with NO. They were questioned by police. It was at the intersection of Calle Agustinas.

"What is going on here, Patricia?"

"University students have a winter vacation. Yesterday's demonstration was the beginning of protests against our government. They say NO to Junta."

"No arrests?"

"Not as much anymore, Señora. Everyone wants peace."

I continued walking in my chosen direction. While crossing the street Huérfanos, I looked ahead and noticed a tall man of an upright posture standing at the entrance of a building on Ahumada Street. I was incredibly drawn to this man, as if his aura captured my own energy field and wouldn't let go. It was an incredibly powerful magnetic vortex that drew me closer to him. Who is he? I asked myself. He is so special! I recognized a familiar bond to this man whose identity was the least of my concerns. Feelings took over me and the guilt entered my mind. No, I cannot look at this man. My husband gave me this trip and he trusts me. I am a married woman. I must not look at this man!

The first effort was quite successful until I came closer. Instead of being forty meters away, I was two meters from him. He was an enigma that fascinated me. It was unexplainable, yet penetrating, powerful and real. His noble features stamped the image of masculine perfection into my mind, almost as matching the blueprint I held perpetually in its memory.

Just one more look and then I'll forget him. I must forget him! I cannot possibly look at him. I am a married woman!

One more treat. What a special face! Manly, rough and gentle, proud and humble. What is he doing here? He is not from here! He was looking into the distance, waiting for someone. I had an affinity with this man who had hardly noticed me!

I remained faithful to my commitment and looked away, aware that Patricia was a silent observer of the mental chat in my divided mind. I passed him by.

A few seconds later, a crowd of pedestrians had dispersed into all directions of the large square called Plaza d'Armas, when I realized where I was.

"I can't believe this, Patricia. The Embassy is in the other direction of Ahumada. How could I get this disoriented?"

"I told you, Señora, but you wouldn't listen!"

"You told me?" I truly couldn't remember. I had no memory of anything that preceded this awakening realization into reality. I totally forgot about the handsome stranger. It was like a sudden awakening after which we forget the dream we just had.

"Yes, I told you! You said you knew where you were going!"

"Strange, I don't know why I did that. Well, let's just go back the same way. We're in no hurry."

Arm in arm, we embarked on the same route, looking ahead for a space to pass between the shoulders of pedestrians. Ahumada is a major downtown passage with no traffic. Only at crossings with other streets some vehicles are rushed through. It is a place where all kinds of people can be seen; the upper, middle and lower class and where beggars and pick-pockets usually get very lucky.

Suddenly, I noticed a group of young religious men walking briskly right in the middle of the passage, to avoid the greater crowd on sidewalks. They attracted my attention.

"Who are these men, Patricia? Are they monks?"

At this instant, Patricia stepped energetically right in front of me, blocking my way and looking sternly into my eyes, she delivered an instant answer.

"They're the priests of the Order of Santa Gemita, Señora Ingrid!"

I stopped. The sound of Patricia's voice bewildered me. She answered with such a certainty and authority! What had come over her? I couldn't recognize this simple country girl! And there was a strange feeling associated with this moment! I felt compelled to look to my left. I knew I was observed. A powerful presence and a magnetic pull drew my attention further to the left and there my eyes met the eyes of the handsome stranger. We were enraptured! I looked straight into his eyes with the wonderment of a child, as if a mythical being appeared before me. Patricia became a witness to something out of this world. She saw us in this rapture for a minute, him looking at me with a hypnotic transport. I saw much more than that. Within seconds, a milky white light began to descend onto his head, spreading its boundaries around him and me, embracing and shielding us in the cocoon shape of an ovum. Pedestrians, who tried to enter this six-foot space between us, bounced off the invisible wall and avoiding our sacred space, they continued walking down the street toward Huérfanos. As the light entered us, he changed his appearance. Suddenly, he had dark hair, beard and brown eyes. In this moment I perceived a clear message from him: I KNOW YOU. YOU ARE PART OF ME. All this time I was breathless and in a blissfully exalted state, locked into his eyes that radiated the deepest confession of love and devotion. With peripheral vision I could see Patricia staring at him, also mesmerized. And then I inhaled; maybe we both inhaled. He and I breathed the white light into us. As we came out of this enchantment, we looked at each other with an evident amazement about what had just happened to us. He had greenish blue eyes now and looked very humble, compared to the self-confident presence he displayed when I saw him first. I scanned him with my gaze. Well groomed, high forehead, prominent nose, sensual lips, masculine chin, all forming a well put together face, handsome and attractive. He wore a woollen calf-length black coat, black slacks and shoes. He held a briefcase in his left hand. He had no ring! Thoughts flooded my mind, my heart pounded while I was looking at this man who would inspire me to the highest I'd be able to accomplish; the one I would cross valleys and oceans for. I rewarded myself with one more glance over his tall body dressed in black. He looked at Patricia in this moment; he blushed and felt slightly embarrassed under my scanning. Then he looked back at me, gasping for the air, ready to say something. At this instant I took Patricia's arm and walked away from him.

An intense lament overwhelmed me. The inner dialogue resumed.

...What am I doing? I cannot walk away like that! I must do something!

I looked back, with a happy smile.

…At the least, that I can do. He is so beautiful! He blushes! Oh, what a pure man! I can see his torso contracting in deep breathing; I can feel his heart beating fast! He smiles! This is heaven!

I stopped for a moment. In nanoseconds, realizations were pouring into my mind.

…He is the one I always loved. What am I going to do? I am a married woman. I cannot talk to him!

Patricia was observing me, saying nothing. She became a witness to the encounter and felt my frustration. We continued walking down the street. I looked back at him one more time to give him a smile he was not to forget. He called me by the name PAMELA. His lips moved and articulated the name Pamela.

I stopped and hesitated. A deep pain entered my heart. It was growing and magnifying. I felt our pain, his and mine. I was dying, dying, dying ….. He was dying with me. We shared one more moment of eye to eye contact, to carry forever in our memory. I had taken into my future the light of his enamoured eyes, the meek smile and his presence in my heart to be able to walk away from him and remain faithful to my commitment. I was a newly-wed woman with family responsibilities. I went against the voice of my heart, divided myself again and separated myself from unity that I was privileged to feel since that early morning. I walked away from the one who was now a part of me and made me whole. The inner struggle resumed until a silent voice said: you will see him again when you both are ready to meet. Go back to your life; complete your life with your family. Keep on walking! You're strong, you can do it!

I did it. I looked only ahead, passing by the demonstrators, looking up to spot a Canadian flag.

"There it is, Patricia! It is on the upper floor. I remember the location now! I was pregnant with Andrew when I was here last time."

"That was four years ago, wasn't it, Señora?"

"Yes, Patricia. We left Chile at that time. Time flies by quickly."

Patricia had to wait in the hallway, while I was allowed to meet an officer inside the Embassy, who provided me with additional information about some manufacturers. It lifted me from a regret I felt about my previous conduct, only for a while, until Patricia and I sat at the hotel's dining room table. The feeling that I perhaps made a terrible mistake obsessed my mind. I had no idea if I entered the Portal of Death, or Rebirth. The echo of the encounter began to haunt me.

Patricia has kept quiet about the incident, until I proposed a toast.

"To this very unique day!" and we clicked our glasses.

Few moments of silence passed till Patricia broke the ice.

"How could you walk away from that man, Señora?"

"I had to. Please, don't make me regret it more than I already do."

"At the least, you could have talked to him! You always talk to people!"

"Duty, Patricia, is a powerful scruple. I have a family. I am a newlywed. I got married only three months ago and my husband trusts me, remember?"

"This man was special! He looked at you in such a powerful way. You must have fallen in love with him!"

"I could speak with any other man, Patricia, but not with this one, just because he was and is so special."

I took a moment to reflect on the day. It was the most magnificent day of my life; it offered the range of feelings and perceptions, the spectrum of energy frequencies, it provided a proof of human multidimensionality and how much can manifest on this Earth when everything is in its place, according to the higher plan. On this busy street of one of the most polluted cities, I have experienced the sacredness of human and divine kinship.

"It will be hard to return to my husband the way I have been with him, but I will try. I must try. Life has to be lived moment to moment; we have to do our best in every instant of it. I did the right thing for the time being, Patricia."

"Who do you think he is?"

"In the real life? I am not sure. He looked like a scholar to me, but I will call him Priest. A very caring and involved man he is. He had manuscripts in his briefcase."

"How do you know that, Señora?"

"I felt it. He writes and teaches and speaks several languages. He communicated to me in English."

Patricia opened her eyes wide, in dismay.

"He said something to you?"

"It was telepathic. He also called me Pamela."

"This is strange, Señora....That man loves you! I could feel it. You are his bride!"

Patricia reminded me how difficult it will be to remain grounded and detached. I cried within me, my heart was torn and my soul quenched. The portal to my altar remained open. If I could only drink of that chalice one more time, look into my Priest's eyes and weave the initiation gown from its golden rays! I truly died to who I was prior to this trip. He died with me.

I sipped some more from the goblet of Chilean red wine, a Merlot or whatever it was. It could not quench the thirst for a communion I longed for from that day on.

"You may never meet this man again, Señora. Why didn't he follow you?"

"He is a respecter of free will. He honoured my choice. Besides, he was waiting for someone. He couldn't leave the location. That person was about twenty minutes late. It was twenty minutes passed three o'clock. He was waiting for a Chilean, obviously."

Patricia laughed, acknowledging a drop of truth about her own people.

"Will you look for him, Señora Ingrid?"

"No matter what it takes, Patricia, I am going to find out who he is and why I met him today. Cheers to my Journey!"

THE DIVINE COMEDY

POPES

I HAD one day just to myself. Patricia had to return to her husband and had to instruct her cousin Roberto where to locate me. I went one more time to the location where I met my Priest, exactly at 15:20, in hope that he might do the same. I was sure that he desired to meet me again.

During the day I wondered how I'd manage to go on in life with strong emotions that were now magnified by his. Our connection was established. In the world of matter we were distanced; in the world of spirit we became accessible. His face was continuously reminding itself on the screen of my third eye. He became my companion. I was new at this, becoming concerned about my daily functionality of being fully present. Positively, my feet were set on the path of discovery, but I needed clarity of mind and balance to get ahead. Never had I intended to become another Don Quijote. Was there a choice, though? I also had to become my own teacher and had to be skeptical as much as possible to remain grounded. I appealed to my inner doubter Thomas for assistance.

In the evening of doing nothing after the first seven days of the creation of my own unresolved puzzle, I had rested. God rested on the seventh day. I was beyond that. Curious about the outside world, I watched the television that became a source of information on that day. The cardinal was already in Chile. I guessed the priests we saw on Ahumada were coming to the Liberation Theology convention. I could almost hear the trumpets of Revelation in the ethers announcing that the change was on its way. What ever was to happen…! We all thrive in changes with great challenges. I was ready with my modest breast plate.

Roberto arrived on the following morning. I met him at the bus terminal and within hours we were on the bus to Mendoza. I gave Roberto the window seat. His father Manuel sat behind me. We seldom talked on the way. Los Andes have very little of the beauty of the Canadian Rockies. Aconcagua seemed insignificant and so was the famous ski resort Portillo. Argentine territory had a couple of interesting highlights, such as a natural formation in the rock on one of the slopes looking like a tiger. And there was Mendoza, the city of tango, exiles, leather and dealers. Everybody knew somebody who had the best prices of leather jackets. After checking two hotels, we had to pick the four-star. It was just comfortable

Roberto had a bed by the window; I had mine by the door. We both shared equal distance to the bathroom that needed extra scraping. The door knob was broken. We simply had to trust each other. Considering that Roberto came along to make sure that I am safe, I trusted.

Tired and hungry, we rushed to look for a fast food place. We found a small restaurant around the corner. Before we took the first bite, two men offered us the best deals in leather. One of them was going to take us there on his motorcycle. I admired his resourcefulness. This was Friday night. I purchased two jackets on Saturday from another dealer.

We reserved the Saturday night for dancing. The nearest Tangomania was within a walking distance. I could hardly wait for the next day, as anxious I became. If you ever danced tango, you may as well fantasize dancing it in Argentina. Well, I did!

In the morning, right after we locked our room door, a group of seven young priests were just turning a corner of our hallway, being led by a cardinal who was blind. He almost touched me with his white cane. He was about forty years old; the priests averaged thirty. For a while I was compelled to say something to the cardinal, but the words had left my tongue and I stood there in silence. All his companions were handsome. Doubtlessly, they looked Spanish. They began to enter a room next to ours, one by one. It had to be a room reserved for Snow White and the Seven Dwarfs. One of the priests couldn't get his eyes off me. He was cute!

Roberto made a comment in the elevator.

"We certainly can be at peace with these neighbours!"

"Roberto, I felt an urge…'

"I could see that!" The young man was far too quick with his answers.

"Let me finish, Roberto!"

I continued the sentence on the way to the dining room.

"I had an urge to speak with the blind man."

"The blind man cannot appreciate you, Señora Ingrid."

"Roberto, I had a message for the cardinal. Let's hope that this trip doesn't represent missed opportunities."

"You have made that mistake once already in Santiago on Wednesday, right?"

"How do you know about it?"

"The first thing Patricia told everyone was about this handsome man whom you fell in love with. Was it really that special?"

"Special is not the correct word. It was divine...."

"Divine? Like Heaven, Paradise?"

"Paradise, Roberto, Paradise."

I reviewed the encounter again. How many more times will I do it?

Luckily the waiter came to take our order right away. I didn't feel hungry anymore. I ordered a continental breakfast. Roberto ordered eggs and ham.

"Let us plan the day, Roberto. First, we shall find out where to get a jacket for my husband. After lunch we're free. What do you want to do?"

"With you? Anything, Señora!"

"We can talk, how about that?" I suggested.

"Yes, we can start with a talk, Señora Ingrid."

I had never seen a man chewing his food as slowly as Roberto had. It was a ritual!

"Has your mother taught you about digestion and assimilation?"

"Not my mother, but my teachers had."

"Who were your teachers, Roberto?"

"Women, Señora, women."

A sensual lad! No wonder he looked so healthy and girls liked him. He was an attractive man. Only twenty-two! He could be my son! He looked more western European than of Chilean roots.

After another ritual of dining at suppertime, it was time to get ready for the night of dancing the tango. We waited for Manuel in the lobby for our seven o'clock tango date. When we heard a car stopping by the entrance, we checked it out. It was a station wagon with the cardinal and priests, all eight of them. How could they fit into the vehicle? Roberto looked at me with a mischievous smile. Nobody was supposed to read our thoughts!

Manuel was late. I was pacing in the lobby back and forth, or standing close to entrance. The cute priest stopped and gave me an evaluating look, while the others walked ahead.

"Don't look at me like that, Father!" I said to him, while he was undressing me in his imagination.

"I am not looking at you like that!" he answers.

"Yes, you are!"

"I am not!"

"Father, I am a mother of five children!"

He glanced briefly at Roberto.

"I see.... how lovely. Congratulations!"

His companions were waiting for him by the elevator and he proceeded to join them. Then they ascended.

Roberto came over and whispered over my shoulder,

"Now you had your chance to speak, Señora. Did you pass him your message?"

A rascal! A character! He does it again!

"I wanted to speak to the blind one!"

"But I told you earlier, Señora, only a seeing man can appreciate you. This one had eyes to see!"

"Do you have ears to hear, Roberto? I guess you do! Then listen to me! Your comments are funny, but, sometimes I am concerned that you might cause me trouble. Remember, God gave you two eyes, two ears, but only one mouth. Think about it!"

Partially, I was to be blamed for this incident. I wore a lovely black dress, black pumps and stockings that I bought in Santiago for tonight's occasion, and I had a satin red rose pinned to my dress that attracted attention. The young priest was himself.

Manuel arrived. We walked together to the nearest Tangomania. The place looked like a barn, only a part of it was covered by a hardwood dance floor. The stage was brightly lit up and a real orchestra played. We danced and danced up to midnight. Then Manuel suggested getting back to the hotel. The air was charged up. He wanted to avoid trouble. We gladly obeyed.

The moment I walked into our hotel room, I kicked off my shoes, feeling a sudden relief.

"Who is going to take a shower first?" I asked.

No answer.

"Roberto, do you want to take a shower now?"

"I need a cold one, Señora."

Roberto was standing in between the closet door, as if he were stuck. I walked over to him. He was flipping pages of a magazine.

"What are you reading? Did you bring this with you?"

All of a sudden, I noticed it was a pornographic magazine. I became upset and reached out to take it from him.

"Give it to me! Where did you get this?"

"It was up here in the closet, Señora."

Roberto was telling the truth. I was thinking about the priests.

"Imagine, Roberto, when priests find it!"

We had good belly laughter. I checked the dresser and the night table drawers.

"What are you looking for, Señora?"

"A Bible! Canadian hotels have Bible in the rooms. Here they have a pornographic magazine!"

We both laughed even more. Roberto agreed to take a bath first. It gave me a chance to look into a confiscated magazine. Even though I was in my third marriage, it was clear to me that I was naïve!

Later, when I finished my bath, Roberto was already asleep in his bed by the window. I turned off the light and thanked God for a day full of fun. I was looking forward to the trip back to Chile in the afternoon. I fell fast asleep.

About one hour later, I heard Roberto's whisper.

"Señora Ingrid, are you asleep?"

"Not anymore! What is it, Roberto?" It takes so little to wake me up. It must be mother's syndrome.

"I cannot sleep!" says a bit louder whisper.

"Pray, then!"

"I already did, Señora!"

"Count the sheep!" I suggested.

"How do you count sheep?"

"One, two, three, and so on, until you run out of sheep!"

"I have never heard of that."

"So count something else. Money, whatever, until you run out of it."

"That would be easy, I ran out of money already!"

"Look, Roberto, I want to sleep. Don't bother me anymore, okay?"

It was easy to figure out what was on Roberto's mind, being a young, healthy and inspired man. That damn magazine spoiled my sleep! Under no circumstances was I going to fall into Roberto's scheme. I was ignorant, innocent and terribly sleepy.

I was near twilight zone when I heard a whisper again.

"Señora, I still cannot sleep."

I pretended that I heard nothing. I was sound asleep. Few minutes passed. I became aware of the time. Roberto was tossing and turning in his bed, and yawning aloud.

"Señora, what shall I do?"

"Count your breath! You never run out of that!"

"Do you think that will work?"

"Guaranteed! It takes you into a meditative state."

"Do you meditate, Señora?"

"No time. I am an activist. I do things."

"I like to do things too, Señora!"

I was becoming agitated. This young fellow never quits! A typical man, keeping on trying until he gets what he wants. No matter what, I had to be on top of the situation.

"Do you want me to sing you a lullaby?"

"Only if I can come to your bed," responded Roberto quickly.

"Forget it! I don't sleep with men."

"Your husband is a man!"

For a moment I was wondering whether our conversation was amusing, or challenging. Roberto didn't insist on this trip. He was invited to keep me company and take me back to Chile in safety. Did he actually believe that he was to look after my needs? Mine were certainly different from his. Regardless, I had to do something to stay out of trouble.

"Roberto, you know you cannot get anywhere this way. You're supposed to be my body guard, not my lover!"

"I am your body guard! I would love to watch over it forever, Señora! You are the woman of my dreams!"

"Good try, Roberto! If you don't smarten up, I am going to call a priest for help!"

"That would not help. One was already undressing you in his mind. And they saw the magazine!"

A flash of inspiration! The magazine! Now I am going to use Roberto's weapon against him. What an opportunity to transform darkness into light! The motif of my favourite fairy tales! Duality interplay is behind all evolution and growth and it was available to me right now!

"Roberto...? Would you like to have an unforgettable experience?" I asked in a very nocturnal seductive voice. I did my best to lower the pitch.

"With you, Señora?" asked excited Roberto.

I observed his breathing. None of us could keep up counting his breaths.

"Under one condition: that you will be a recipient, and I will be a giver."

"Oh, Señora! You are such a beautiful and giving woman!"

"The rule is that the recipient cannot touch the giver. You must be submissive."

"This is the dream of my life!"

Quickly, I had to gather all resources from my imagination in the domain of lust. I had to think what Roberto would like the most. It had to be like a perfectly wrapped package, with bows and ribbons, with many layers of paper, and if possible, having many scotch tapes, waiting to be opened slowly. Inside had to be a real surprise, such as a gift certificate or a rain cheque.

First, I asked Roberto to stay in a supine position on his bed and make sure he felt comfortable. Then I energetically stripped the top sheet of my bed and glided it in front of my body. A special emphasis on sensuality had to be considered at all times. I rolled the sheet into a thick rope, placed it across Alberto's hips, and tied it together on the side of the bed. The final knot was completed when Roberto inhaled. He was left to count his breath after all. I used my winter coat to keep warm and observed the tamed Roberto from my bed, beginning to feel a genuine compassion for him. He gave me a gift of this unusual experience I cannot possibly forget, unless, I chose to.

"Good night, Roberto!"

"Your husband has a treasure in you. A lucky man!"

Roberto surrendered; no more whispers. I hoped to sleep four hours. We had to return to Santiago by the afternoon bus.

It must have been near noon hour when I woke up. I phoned reception. It was eleven. I ordered breakfast through a room service. Roberto was asleep. I had a little hangover from the cigarette smoke in Tangomania place. In a short while, there was a knock on the door. I buttoned my coat and barefoot went to open the door. The same young waiter, who served us each time, cheerfully wished me "Good morning." His facial expression changed quickly when he saw Roberto tied to his bed. Angrily, the waiter put the tray on the dresser, attempting to wake Roberto up with the impact.

"Enjoy your scrambled eggs!" he said angrily and left.

Roberto woke up. He said no word about the last night. I untied him and gave him a breakfast on the tray.

"Aren't you going to share it with me, Señora?" he humbly asked.

"I'll wait for our early dinner. The bus leaves at four. I am not hungry yet."

Slowly, I began to get our things ready and took plenty of time in the bathroom. Roberto was respectful and not very chatty. Poor lad, he learned his lesson.

We were the only guests in the dining room. The waiter came to take our order.

"What would Señora like? We can have the chef to prepare a special dish."

"Lots of vegetables and hardly any meat. Actually, a broth would be appreciated."

"What ever you desire, Señora!" said the waiter in a very subservient manner.

Then he moved over to Roberto, whom he ignored up to then, stepped with one foot in front of the other, looked at him sternly and with superiority in his voice said,

"And what would the kid like? A glass of milk?"

Roberto was shocked. Him, who was treated yesterday with courtesy, became a second class citizen overnight.

I had to interfere.

"The young man can order for himself. I am sure that chef can prepare something special for him as well."

The waiter bowed to me while saying "Whatever you say, Señora!"

Then the waiter turned to Roberto and in the tone he used earlier he suggested,

"How about a chicken breast and thighs with sauce to satisfy your appetite?"

"An excellent suggestion! Make sure the meat is of a young and fresh chicken. Custard for dessert, please!"

A defeated waiter left, with the orders. Roberto looked at me,

"Are you enjoying yourself, Señora? He thinks I am a gigolo!" Roberto waited for my input.

"You had a good answer for him," I said with neutrality.

Then we talked a bit - insignificant comments of simple people. No bitterness, no reminders of the past. When plates were cleared, a waiter asked me about a dessert. I told him I will pass on it, that I had plenty of delicious treats to enjoy in the past few days and, asked for the bill. There were no more emotions coming from the waiter. He got a tip he deserved.

We boarded the bus for Santiago. Roberto got his seat by the window; I sat next to him. There were about twenty passengers among whom I noticed a young priest. He carried a very small suitcase and kept to himself. After a couple hours of the bus ride, Roberto reached for the chocolate bars we purchased at a kiosk and passed me two of them. I gave one to the priest who was sitting right across the aisle. At first, he refused with thanks, but when I insisted that he must accept it, he did.

"All good things are much nicer when they're shared, don't you think, Father?" I said to make him feel more comfortable.

"I agree.... Have you enjoyed your stay in Mendoza?"

Roberto looked at me, waiting for my answer. I gave him a glance acknowledging his concern, turning to the priest again.

"Yes, it was an interesting visit. Are you from here, Father?"

"No, Señora, I am a Chilean, but I have a parish here."

"Why here, why not in Chile?"

"They need me here."

I noticed sadness in his voice.

"I can see that. I saw a cardinal with his companions. Have you met them?"

All of a sudden the priest became agitated. "You saw a false Pope!" he said.

"A false Pope? You mean there is a real Pope?"

"Of course, there is a real Pope: Juan Pablo Segundo!"

"Who is he, where is he from?" I asked.

"From the Vatican!" The young priest became impatient with me.

"The blind man?"

"Our Pope is not blind! He can see!" Now the priest was annoyed. I had to heal our misunderstanding immediately.

"Father, I was asking about the man with the white cane. The one I saw!"

"The man is crazy!" said the priest quickly.

"Which man is crazy?"

"The blind one!"

Roberto changed his seating position, looking directly at both of us, waiting for more entertainment. The master of the word riddle became our grateful audience.

"Why is he crazy, Father?"

"He saw Christ!"

"And that makes him crazy?"

"Nobody can see Christ!"

"Nobody can, Father?" I could hardly believe my ears.

"Only our Pope can see Christ!"

"Which one? The blind one or the seeing one?"

"Our Holy Father, Juan Pablo Segundo!"

The priest began to look away into the window. I had no idea that a chocolate bar would start all this. I was determined to find out why the blind cardinal carried stigmata of insanity and, what happened. Also, I had to consider the young priest's devotion toward hierarchy of the Catholic Church. Roberto gave me an encouraging twinkle in his eye and a more obvious push into my arm.

"Father, God is not a respecter of persons. Sun shines on everyone. Sometimes a blind person can see what a seeing person would not notice. Blindness can be a gift, so can a naiveté be a gift. Do you understand what I am saying?"

There was a moment of silence. The priest knew that I wanted to continue in our awkward dialogue.

"Señora, this crazy cardinal went to Vatican to claim the office of Papacy. He said to our Holy Father that Christ has chosen him for a Pope."

"That takes courage, don't you think?"

"A fool! Holy Father demanded an apology, but the fool would not take his claim back. So, he was excommunicated. Now he is on a crusade against our Holy Father."

"Courage of this kind comes from the Spirit."

"Devil made him do it!" said the priest with repulse and crossed himself, remaining in silence for a while.

I gave him all the time he needed to calm himself down. He was so young, about twenty-eight. His features were refined; his medium height body was dressed in a navy blue habit. He would make a perfect husband to some girl. So many women in South America dream about a man like him.

"Are you going to visit your family, Father?" I asked a while later.

"Yes, I am going to baptize my new niece."

"How lovely! My four children were baptized in Chile. The priest's name was Padre Salvador. What's your name, Father?"

"Raul. And what is yours, Señora?"

"Ingrid... Ingrid Heller!"

"A pleasure to meet you!"

"The same here." I nodded my head and smiled at him. He felt more at ease. I captured this moment to continue in our discussion.

"Have you heard of duality, Father Raul?"

"Duality? Like male and female, good and evil, Heaven and Hell?"

"Black and white, light and darkness, negative and positive...." I collaborated.

"Yes! Why are you asking, Sister?"

"That was excellent! You called me Sister, my Brother! One without the other doesn't have a meaning. There must be contrasts and opposites in everything. Their interplay leads to action toward progress. It all comes from one Source - Unity. It is good for your Holy Father to have an opposition. This false Pope can teach him more than anyone else. Do you know what I mean, Brother Raul?"

I could see in his eyes that he was trying to comprehend, thinking about my words.

"Brother Raul, we are One in the human family. All of us are sharing this Planet. We must be here for some reason. We are here to learn something, right?"

"Yes, to accept Jesus Christ as our Saviour," was Raul's instant response.

I resumed in my intent.

"Jesus was a good teacher and example. He always said: 'I am the way'. He never rejected anyone. He healed those who came to him to be healed and asked us to love each other the way He loved us. He taught us to love our enemies. He embraced the darkness by descending to Hell. It says in your Credo! He redeemed the World with all that there is, including the opposites. Once we learn to understand our opposites, there is no more darkness and no more secrecy. In the beginning and at the end all is united. Only in the middle it is divided. Creation is perfect, Brother Raul!"

"Because our Father in Heaven is perfect."

Raul's eyes kept on following the silhouette of the Cordillera. He was at peace with himself now and I was truly happy for him. I left him alone. Suddenly, I heard a soft snore next to me. It was Roberto. I placed his new leather jacket over his shoulders and observed him for a while. As long as there was a controversy in the dialogue, he followed with his mind. The latter subject must have become boring to him. Frequently I wondered what kind of a woman would marry Roberto. There are many many more women than men in South America, a true phenomenon. He might stay single, enjoying them all.

My mind had taken on its wings and I was back on Calle Ahumada, near Huérfanos, seeing my Priest-King. I was quite anxious to share the spiritual depth of my encounter with someone. Frankly, I wasn't even sure that my best friend Hanna would believe it. Despite her wisdom, she'd be skeptical. Probably my old friend Ray would be open to it. He was well-read in esotericism. I knew that my friend Aaron would appreciate it! He is always neutral and gives the most sincere feedback. He comes from oneness. I was looking forward to my return to Santiago. Maybe I'll see my Priest again, if good luck would have it. I was contemplating a trip to Concepción. Somehow I felt I should be there.

I must have fallen asleep. A gentle touch on my shoulder woke me up. It was Father Raul.

"Sister, I am very happy I have met you. I will always remember you."

I could feel a sorrow of parting again. I stood up and gave him a hug. He was open to it.

"May Peace be with you, Brother Raul..."

He walked toward the front door, giving me one more glance before descending the steps. He blushed slightly. Roberto was awake, watching "chicas" boarding our bus.

"Señora, the priest is looking back here. He is waving to you! You must have impressed him!"

I waved back to Raul, who was already on another bus. This stop was in Los Andes, the major crossroads. It was the town of the legendary Santa Teresa de Los Andes.

Roberto must have gotten tired of 'new chics', looking at my reflected image in the window now. It was dark outside and the driver kept the dimmed lights on.

"You surely have a crush on Priests, don't you, Señora Ingrid!?" said Roberto.

"I like them innocent, Roberto, I like them innocent...."

Three hours later, he transferred to the bus to his town. He thanked me for the trip, my company and the jacket. He said it all in an Argentine accent. I went back to the hotel Libertador, planning the next few days. I didn't have much time left in this country. Married or not, I was determined to find out who my Priest was, if he was a priest.

CONCEPCION

INSTEAD of sitting in a lotus position and meditating on the subject "Quest for my Priest", to get his name, address and phone number, I searched in a dimension of time and space. Since it was the world I knew the best and my mind couldn't play tricks on me in the tangible reality, I felt totally comfortable about what I was doing. When Don Quijote de la Mancha found his sweetheart, his image of the perfect female was crushed. The image of my male was perfectly all right with me. He was handsome and attractive and I could describe his features at any time to anyone. Only, I could not draw his image. Me, who used to draw portraits, could not portray his face on paper. A combination of the Nordic and Jewish features is hard to draw. His face, the masque, was so familiar, that I began to ponder whether I'd seen him somewhere after all.

Let's suppose that he was a priest. Patricia mentioned The Order of Santa Gemita. I inquired. No one of the described features was a part of the Chilean Santa Gemita group. The next step was the office of the archbishop. Apparently, the registry had no photographs of priests. I was afraid to talk about Jesus Christ's image. They might have told me that only John Paul II can look like that. The archbishop was out of town at a very important meeting. I figured they planned their strategy of how to "overthrow" the government. Junta members were regular at masses and probably generous in donations. How could anyone bite the hand that feeds them? Favours from God cannot be bought; they have to be earned. When Church is bought, it can be bought by anyone. It cannot be trusted. There is always someone who plays the Almighty anonymously.

My next destination was Concepción in the middle of Chile. I took with me Patricia's mother. Señora Rosa was a country woman with ladylike manners. We liked each other and enjoyed conversing together.

We arrived at Concepción on Friday, the 22nd of July, the Saint Magdalene's Day. The city is well known for its university surrounded by a lovely park and, for its leathers and textiles.

We checked into a hotel, hired a taxi driver and went on. First, we shopped for wools. It had to be pure virgin. We found it in every store. We got a good deal.

In the morning, a room service slid a newspaper under our hotel room door. Señora Rosa picked it up and started to read.

"Señora Ingrid, the cardinal meets with the representatives of the Church here in Concepción today!"

"It sounds like a conception of something! Does it say where?"

"No, it does not!" answered Señora Rosa sadly.

One hour later, we asked our friendly taxi driver. He took us to the office of Alejandro Goic-Karmelic, the big boss of the Church. His nun secretary had no information for us. The taxi driver was curious why we wanted to know about the meeting. We had to tell him some of the truth. He believed that one of the priests of the nearby Lotta matched the description. He drove us there. On the way he pointed out a location where a school bus had an accident and many children died. Since then, when anyone stops there, people hear voices of children calling for their family members. No one likes to stop there anymore.

Lotta was a small town where people heat their homes by burning coals and tires. It smelled bad. I walked alone to the parish building of a mustard yellow colour. An older priest of tall stature received me. I asked for a younger one. He said they were working. When I asked him if any of the younger priests were in Santiago on July thirteenth, he became agitated. He denied it. It was obvious that he suspected I was some kind of agent or investigator. There was no way he would trust me. Then I had an idea.

"Father, I'd like to confess..."

"The mass is over, Señora Heller."

"But I sinned, Father!"

"Sorry, I cannot help you!" he answered calmly, walking me to the door.

Before I walked into the street, I turned to him, giving him a note with our hotel's phone number and asked if he could call me later. He said he had nothing to talk about.

It was obvious that I messed up. The taxi driver had another idea. He knew that Señor Goic-Karmelic was a kind and sensitive person; therefore, he believed if I'd write him a letter, I might get some answer later on. I wrote a one page note right in the taxi. The same lovely secretary promised to pass the letter to the Señor.

We were dropped off in the hotel and prepared for our return. We hoped to receive a phone call, but in vain.

We left Concepción the following morning and on the way encountered a very thick fog. The experienced bus driver was delayed only one hour.

My departure for Canada was nearing and I had accomplished hardly anything in my search. I decided to postpone my flight one week. I didn't contact all the people I wanted to be in touch with and yet, had more business to take care off.

Before returning to Santiago, I wanted to spend couple of days in the countryside where we lived up to four years ago. Señora Rosa made sure that one of their bedrooms was still available to me. They used to be our neighbours and the walk from their place toward the land we owned was only fifteen minutes.

I hoped for some revelation through a dream and I prayed to be guided to the people who could assist me. I needed to open many doors and wait for the first indications of a successful search. Time mattered no more. I was prepared to give it all and had given conception to many ideas.

HOPE

SIX years earlier I had no idea why I moved to Chile or where it was eventually going to lead. I believed in the South American continent and a Chilean future. Despite the present political situation, in my heart I knew that this was a country of hope.

The afternoon in the countryside was quite pleasant. My destination was my ex-residence. The weather was good and the road was comfortably passable. I looked ahead into Cordillera de la Costa and its highest peak. There were gold mines in the area, which perhaps explained frequent UFO sightings. Everyone in the area had seen them a few times, at the least. I chose not to go into my memories. They were mostly painful. I kept on filling my lungs with the purity of country air, inhaling on the count of five, holding it for nine seconds, and exhaling slowly. My walking pace slowed down. I was peaceful, grateful; I was joyous. This country offered me a range of human experience I could not have had anywhere else. Is there more to come? The future is fascinating when we don't know what it brings. And we have the power to create it! Human beings must be made well, if we can be trusted with the process of creating. We must be made in God's image and mind. We must be a well-premeditated experiment! Do we really have a free will? If we do, up to what point, then? And what happens after we complete with our and God's will? Do we go beyond that and become co-creators with God? What happens to the evolution of matter and spirit? Who is responsible for what? If the human being is entrusted with the blueprint of creation and evolution, then it is up to the human being to bridge action from one point to the other. Only by winding stairs we can climb the tower. We cannot possibly envision the greatness of our mission, however small it may be!

I felt loved and began to realize how important my little existence was and that there was only one like me. There was no a duplicate of Ingrid Heller anywhere in the vast Universe. I had to learn to trust my inner guidance more and literally follow my heart. I had the most powerful tool - I was in love. I met my match. His blueprint and map to Kingdom had to be similar to mine, if not identical. Yet, his lifetime experiences had to be different from mine. We were independent from each other, but shared each other during our blessed encounter. What would happen if we got together on that day? Would we stay together? A man like him should have at least one copy of himself! I wished to be the mother of his offspring. This thought was extremely tempting. I desired to find my Adam soon. At this point, I was certain that I had to take it step by step. The major event had already taken place - I've met him. The next step was gathering information that would lead me to him. Or, shall I simply dismiss him from my mind and trust that he'll appear again? At this point, I wouldn't dare to do that. I needed to nurture the action with my thoughts and feelings of love. Every time I rewound my tape of memory, I experienced the same exalted feeling I had when I met him. I kept on playing the tape many times a day. I knew that he has been doing the same. As a matter of fact, I was aware that it was me who had to find him. It wasn't his responsibility. If Eve started all the "trouble" leading into exile, it had to be Eve again to bring her Adam back to Eden. Descent into the world of duality must have been a painful experience of separation. Now we were ascending, coming into Unity. Naturally, I was to succeed in my search of my beloved and the Paradise we were promised. A new hermaphrodite, the balanced being in male and female polarities was to emerge. Exciting times, indeed!

Nothing could hold me too long in the countryside. I was anxious to return to Santiago and stir up some action before my departure. I visited with all my ex-neighbours who kept on asking about my family's return to Chile. I could only promise them a visit. The marriage to my Canadian husband did not allow me the freedom to move to another country. Señora Rosa predicted my return based on my encounter and her family dared to prophesy much greater possibilities. We parted in a very cordial way.

Prior to leaving their humble country home, I went to their garden to a grotto with sculpture of Virgin Mary. I prayed Love Rosary beads once - not the catholic mysteries and the tiring repetition of Hail Mary. I liked the mantra of Love Rosary, while keeping on rolling the beads between my fingers. Interestingly, Rosa's German shepherd dog observed me from a distance. Not once had she disturbed my meditation. She was as perceptive as her mother Sheba was.

The hotel Libertador became my home till the day of my departure. This room was more comfortable and had a four-piece bathroom. The Libertador room was like a springboard for further action. For a while, I thought of planning a strategy to instigate my search, but it didn't feel right. I chose to follow my heart and intuition instead.

I went for a walk into the Ahumada passage. It was crowded, as usual. The corner with Huérfanos (which means Orphans) seemed different this time. The Paradise was gone - my other half was not there. I kept on walking and noticed a young charming man at my right keeping a pace with mine. He smiled at me. I walked toward the cathedral, up the stairs, and entered. He followed. Could this be a coincidence? I hoped he was not a priest! I disappeared behind a pillar inside the cathedral to see if he was following me. He waited by the entrance. I had to pass by him on the way out. He might be my messenger! I addressed him.

"What would you like to talk about, little brother?"

He was pleased and immediately responded,

"Do you have a little time for a coffee? I'd like to talk to you."

"What about, little brother?"

"Francisco! My name is Francisco."

He had a pleasant appearance. I felt very comfortable around him.

"My name is Ingrid!"

"German?"

"Canadian. But my background is partially German."

We entered a busy coffee shop nearby. He kept on looking into my eyes and spelled out a question. "Are you married?"

"Yes, I am. How about you?"

"Single. Is your marriage working out? Aren't you planning a divorce? I am very attracted to you." His words poured out at me.

I must have blushed. I remembered this line. It's always the same. I gave Francisco a meek smile in appreciation of his compliment.

"Francisco, you should have no problem finding yourself a wife. There are so many pretty girls in this country who are looking for a charmer like you. Be patient! The right one will come along!"

"But they're not spiritual!"

"How can you tell? Walking into a church indicates absolutely nothing about person's spirituality. Truly spiritual people seldom go to church," I assured him.

"You are truly spiritual, Ingrid. I can see it!"

I paused for a while. His eyes remained gazing into mine, but he also looked through me and around me.

"Francisco, you could be my son!" I introduced him to some of the truth. "You need a young woman who could give you children!"

Francisco continued looking at me in the same way. He had eyes to see. Has my beloved Priest also had eyes to see? I began to appreciate Francisco's presence and invited him for supper at the hotel.

He came. We had a great conversation. He was a spiritual lad, loved Greek and romantic poets and had a healthy flow of thought - he was a natural philosopher in his early twenties. We agreed to see each other before my departure.

There were other people whom I wanted to meet. I followed on it. In this case, I had the address. I was a total stranger to them, yet they welcomed me as if they knew me. Actually, I felt slightly intimidated by their special treatment. Their teenage son was a renowned poet and the host of some television shows. I was naturally curious about his talent and also about my role in his life. The lad's father described to me dreams he had, in which I appeared to them. Dreams are mostly genuine guidance, once we work with them. I chose to leave some room for doubt. During the course of our absolutely magnificent conversation, I had to acknowledge that there was some special ingredient that produced a sweet sensation in our bodies. At times, we could all see a white fog in the room of their house. We formed a circle, holding hands, and thanked the Creator for our special time together. Then the mother of the young man went to look for something and returned with a flat black velvet box. She told me it was for me. I opened it. In it was a golden key about eleven centimetres long and a small tablet with an engraved dedication from a television network for the participation in their programmes during 1982. The key was to the door of the Catholic University in Santiago. Diplomatically, I attempted to give this precious gift back to them. It was their son's and not many people received this award. They all insisted I must accept it. I had no choice.

When I asked why this gift, the boy's mother explained to me what preceded.

"Sister Ingrid, I felt that I must give you something to remember us by, and went into my son's room. Thinking of what it should be, this box fell off the top shelf of my son's bookcase onto my head. It is a gift for you. You must accept it. This key is for you, not for my son!"

I gratefully accepted, but I felt like a custodian of this reward and decided to return the gift to them at some point in the future.

We were naturally curious about each other, sharing information for several hours. They believed I had some mission in Chile and when I told them about my encounter with my Priest, they immediately thought of a priest from the Schønstat Brotherhood who had the qualities I described. This priest's name was Father Christian and he spent a lot of time with their son.

I met with the young poet's family two more times before my departure. They assisted me with the exorcism at our former residence on one occasion.

The following day, I went to the Schønstat retreat that was located in the Florida district of Santiago. Father Christian had been transferred to Ecuador, I was told. If he visited Santiago, he would call his Brothers.

I left crying, counting days. I had only three days left. Then I realized that during that time I could accomplish the impossible, meet new messengers, have a revealing dream, or speak to gods. Only I had to remind myself not to lose the hope and faith in the perfect order of events.

Santiago is the name for St. James, the apostle of Hope. He was the brother of Christ, part of his inner circle, together with Peter and John. I've met my beloved in the perfect place on the perfect day in the country shaped as a sword. The Andes are considered to be the spine of the planet, with Tierra del Fuego at its base and the turbulent Straits of Magellan. Volcanic activity and earthquakes became a part of Chilean life. Those who are thinking of our planet as the living body would appreciate the analogy of base chakra and sexual currents, the force of kundalini and power of love. The force has to be liberated, just like the consciousness of South American people. Did they hold the key to planetary liberation? Wouldn't that explain the social, economic and political struggle they were going through?

It was time to leave. There were a few tremors the night before my flight. I got a seat by the window near the wings. After the take off, I looked into the darkness of this enormous city of four and half millions, illumined by street lights at night. I left behind the deepest of human experiences that connected me eternally to this country. I had to come back! I could not imagine leaving for good. Yes, there will be a time when I will return, or at least, I had Hope.

RECORDS

MY family was waiting for me at the airport. How precious are our children! Andrew and Maria asked immediately about the gifts I promised them. Joe gave me a sweet hug. Jean was as usual - absolutely neutral and detached. Monica welcomed me back and passed me the house key with the words, "It's in your hands now, Mom!" Verne was all dressed up, as he used to be for our dates of dancing and laughter. He granted the children exclusivity to greet me first, while observing me at all time. It was his turn to greet me. No hug, no kiss. His words penetrated through my bones,

"You've changed, Ingrid!" He was worried. I could see it.

"I know I've changed. I need three weeks to ground myself and all will be the way it was before the trip. Give me time."

"I would rather lose you to ten men than to this one!" he replied and said nothing more on the way home.

I wondered how much did he know. Has he had a revealing dream, or sensed the change? Was I really so different that he assumed I must have fallen in love with someone else? Verne was quite an intuitive man. I didn't give him any sound reason about my delayed flight, except phoning him that I'll be one week late. I had to become watchful over my thoughts. Telepathy is a natural phenomenon among family members. No one was supposed to know about the encounter. My friend Hanna and Ray would tell no one. They could be trusted. Frankly, I was anxious to tell them about my trip.

The family evening was nurturing. The children did well while I was away. Joe worked with Verne on most of days and Monica kept the household running smoothly. She was only eighteen years old. Four-year old Andrew stayed mostly in company of his six-year old sister Maria. Thirteen year old Jean was independent. She liked to read, play piano and she probably helped Monica with chores. The vegetable garden was looked after well. Joe told me about his summer job with great pride. Everyone liked the gifts I brought them. Verne admired the craftsmanship on the leather jacket. We felt peaceful being together again. I described to the children the changes in our past neighbourhood of the Chilean countryside. They were sad to hear about Sheba's death. Most of my pictures were developed in Santiago. The children recognized everyone and were happy to hear that nobody forgot them.

Verne fortunately didn't insist on intimacy. In two days he left for a long trucking trip to the U.S.A. Joe stayed home this time. He needed a vacation. The fourteen year old that looks like a child needs to sleep in sometimes.

I phoned Hanna. She wasn't home the following day either. She probably went camping with her five children. Ray was home. He was very happy to hear from me. His first question was about the fear of death I had prior to my trip. I told him about the encounter.

His reply turned into a question. "What will you do when you find your Priest?"

I had no answer.

He stated that I wasn't ready for him yet, but promised me that he'd try to get some information for me in his meditation. Since I've known Ray for the last ten years, he's been doing the same thing: meditating many hours a day and keeping records of all his experiences. I never asked what his experiences were about, but he claimed that he was working with angels. He was very particular about the secrecy. During his life of sixty-two years he never married or dated. He was introduced to me by a mutual friend, who was an inventor. Ray had some good feedback for me in the past. On occasions it was out of this world. He had absolutely no idea what a family life or a marriage was all about. He had difficulty understanding the realistic aspects of relationships. He admired the writings of Rudolf Steiner and actually, thanks to Ray's influence, I got involved in anthroposophy and often discussed various issues of Steiner's teachings with him. He liked that. When I visited Goetheannum in Dornach near Basel in Switzerland, I could appreciate the greatness of Rudolf Steiner's work. That place is the living testimonial itself, revealing the Mystery of mysteries: the Holy Grail mystery.

I phoned my friend Aaron for an appointment. He is a well-known Akasha reader and has helped me in the past. Aaron was not a fortune teller. As a matter of fact, he never talked about the future. He talked about the present and its relationship to past lives. He helped thousands to understand themselves and those around them better.

Aaron's office was very bright. The decor included plants, paintings and images of symbols. There was always a bit of fragrance. He was happy to see me and gave me one of his great hugs. He couldn't stop smiling. Did he notice something?

"You have changed, Ingrid.... you have grown...... your trip was a gift to your life. I am very happy for you! Any questions?"

"Aaron, I met this man on July 13th right in the heart of Santiago. We experienced a rapture together that lasted several seconds and during that time he transmitted information to me about the two of us. I walked away from him because of my marriage, but later I regretted it. I want to find him again. I need help, Aaron. Can you collaborate on it, please?"

While I was speaking, Aaron closed his eyes. He breathed a few times deeply through his nose and hummed in a high pitch for a while. After a few more breaths he began to read from the Record of my Soul.

"What we see here is a pattern of heresy in the late thirteen hundreds. He was a teacher in the movement of Rosicrucianism and you were one of the students. He admired your wisdom and made you an equal partner in teachings and then in life. Your gift was that of healing. You healed many and people came to you from far away. It worried your partner because the Church began to inquire about you. Eventually, he used this opportunity to challenge the Church about their healings. As a result of that you were burned at the stake. He still feels guilty about it. He wants to be protective of you this time and doesn't want to involve you in his stream of life activity. He'd rather stay away from you than lose you...... In other lives you were his inspiration. Many times he was with someone else, but loved you. You always got together at the most important times of history. You also died together a few times."

I was silent for a while, feeling the echo of Aaron's words that resonated inside me. He was telling me the truth.

"Is he a priest?" I asked.

"He cares about people, speaks on behalf of the oppressed. There were many missing in South America. He is involved with that movement. He keeps some records."

"Where is he, Aaron?"

"He is from around there."

"How will I find him, Aaron?"

"You've already found him. Through those eyes you established an eternal connection. He recognized you."

"Does he want me to find him again?"

"He has work to do. A family life would be in the way. Humanity is his family. Look, Ingrid you have young children, a husband who loves you. That is your life now! That is your job. Let the other man go. Set him free! Do that for him and for yourself..... "

Aaron looked at me with gentle kindness. At this point I wasn't ready to hear what he was saying. I understood the importance of detachment and preferred to be that way, but I wanted to find my Priest again. What if he needs me? I might be able to help him with his work! What if he gets ill and has no one to take care of him? Regardless of the reading, I had to find out on my own who my Priest was. I didn't want to tell Aaron all the details about our encounter. It was far too sacred to me at this time. I wouldn't tell anyone about my special spiritual experiences, either. I had to keep pearls to myself.

"I am proud of you, Ingrid, that you conquered your fear of dying and went on the trip anyway."

"I think I died on that street when I parted from him. We both died."

"Dying is part of living. If you want to learn how to live fully, you have to learn how to die first. Every day you should repeat this process. That's what the carrying of the cross is all about. Some complain and pity themselves. Let them be then, walking in the same circle, getting nowhere. Crucifixion is for the kings, for the best of the crop!"

Aaron paused for a while and gave me time to contemplate what he just said to me. "Since I've known you, Ingrid, you never complained about your hardships. Each time you come to see me, you are empowered and enriched. You always managed to transform the present situation into a higher one. You are always one step ahead of yourself. You have a power in your name. Heller - the one of the light, the one with halo. Ingrid is another. INRI was engraved on the cross!"

"Doesn't it mean 'Jesus of Nazareth, the King of Israel?" I asked quickly.

"That is an explanation of the uninitiated ones. It has much greater significance. It is the secret to alchemy, the old hermetic science of transmutation. Seek, and you shall find. You are an alchemist already."

"What is the most important message you would have for me right now, Aaron?"

"Your throat has to be developed. I can hear you singing with much greater power. Will you sing again?"

"I am considering auditioning for the Bach Chamber Choir. I love baroque music."

"You were a boy soprano at that time. You actually knew Johann Sebastian Bach in person. I wouldn't be surprised that his music will open another door for you. Keep on singing; heal the constriction in your throat. Liberate the speech, so wisdom can be expressed in words."

"Is my Priest a singer too?"

"He might be. He is of Logos, a powerful speaker! But don't worry about him. You are to focus on yourself."

Aaron gave me more information about my children and our relationships. It was very interesting and I could relate to that. The reading and hour were over. The entire session was taped and I could hardly wait to listen to it again at home when I'd have some private time.

It was easy to part with forty-year old Aaron. He was so detached and neutral. Not once did I feel from him a judgement or any unpleasant emotion. He loved his work and he was very good at it.

Hanna came back from her vacation. She was so anxious to hear about my trip, she rushed over to my place the following day to hear Aaron's reading, see photographs from Chile and to see me. I was still in that radiant state and my body felt pregnant.

The children were busy playing together. Hanna had five children, but brought with her only the three youngest ones, who were compatible in ages with Maria and Andrew.

We both listened attentively to the tape and discussed many possibilities. Hanna was excited about my trip experience and helped with a good suggestion.

"Why do you believe that he was a visitor? In Chile there are immigrants from many countries. The German and Jewish communities must be strong there. Chile was not involved in WWII. Your ex-husband might know about him! Ask him! We always come back to the same conclusion that the world is small."

"I just remember, Hanna. My "ex" went to a private school founded and operated by Belgian priests in the area of Providencia, which is next to downtown. I am going to phone him tonight about it. Hey, thanks!"

"Remember, there is always a solution to every problem we're facing. Life is never hard on us. Things happen because we are ready for them."

"I agree, Hanna. Life is presenting us with issues we have matured to solve."

We chatted about many other subjects, mostly related to our children. Later on in the afternoon, we took the children to a spacious playground in the district. It faced west with the magnificent Rockies and we could observe the calm flow of the Bow River in the valley below. When the children got tired of swinging, Hanna and I took over and enjoyed the exciting feeling rushing up our spine, bringing the memories of childhood, nurturing the child within.

Later on that night, I phoned my Chilean ex-husband Eduardo, asking him about the teachers at the Notre Dame School. I described the features of my Priest and received an astonishing answer. The founding priest was of a very high stature, but passed away in recent years. There was another one, also tall, who taught French and Religion, who looked very much like my Priest, according to my description. I asked more about him. I could identify many resemblances. That same night I wrote a letter to the school with a request for Father Jacob's address. I mailed it registered the next day.

During the same week, I obtained a card from Concepción from Señor Alejandro Goic-Karmelic with Padre Christian's address to Ecuador. I was thrilled! One more person believed that I'd met Father Christian. I wrote him a letter on the same day, mentioning the time of my encounter with a brief description of what happened. I asked Father Christian to answer me if there was any affiliation with him. I also sent this letter by registered mail.

Hanna and I kept on phoning each other daily. She became involved in my search very deeply and sometimes had a dream on my behalf. Nothing led to an answer. Ray became critical toward my search. He openly told me that if I found my "man" soon, we would likely end up in bed and would never want to see each other again. He felt it would be better never to find him and rather keep the romance on a higher level, without any physical contact.

What did Ray know about love, anyhow? He obviously spoke from his own experience that must have been very basic. Would this explain his ascetic life denying his own sexuality? A suppressed sexuality is a suppressed expression of the life force, of the healing and creative energy that eventually leads to genius in a human being. Now I was clearer on the meaning of "master bed", or the "lectus genialis". If Ray's opinion would be correct, Romans would call the bed "lectus genitalis" and the English would call it "mastur bate". I considered Ray just a little challenge.

Virgo

THE children were wonderful and easy-going over the summer. Many times we went to the playground above the river valley, where I felt free in my child-like day-dreaming, thinking of fairy tales, about the magical kiss of pure love that interrupted a deep sleep and everyone became alive in the kingdom again.

One early afternoon the door bell rang. It was the mailman. He had a registered letter for me from Ecuador. I perspired while signing for it. My hands turned cold and I began to tremble. I rushed into the kitchen to open the envelope. I read the well spread handwriting:

"Señora Ingrid! I was very pleased to read about your experience in Santiago. I have never seen an angel myself, but firmly believe that some of them live among us. At the time of your encounter, I was in Ecuador. I pray that you will find what you are looking for. You may maintain in correspondence with me, if you wish. I keep very busy with my work, but am able to find some time for myself. Blessings! Father Christian."

A cold wave swept over me. One door of hope had to be closed. I was holding Christian's letter, inhaling its fragrance. I also kept the writing paper to special people in a box with fragrance. His fragrance was musk, emanating a masculine energy. I thanked him for his answer on the feminine rose scented paper.

We kept in written contact for all these years. Later, it narrowed to a Christmas card, but Christian held a balance for me that I needed so much at that time. I hope there will be a day when the two of us will meet and I'll thank him personally for his sensitivity and kindness. I had no answer from the Notre Dame School. No news is good news - I had hope. Many times a day I repeated the Santiago encounter in my mind. It maintained the intensity of our connection; it magnified the energy. Was Father Christian suggesting that I might have seen an angel? When I thought about it, I was indeed looking at my Priest with a child-like wonder, which I experienced in my early childhood when on St. Nicolas' Day my parents hired actors from the theatre in angel's, devil's and St. Nicolas' costumes. I met supernatural beings! My attention was focused entirely on the angel and St. Nicolas. These were powerful moments. I was only two at that time. Two years later, when I already sinned a little, all my attention went to the devil, whose costume was so complete, that he had hooves, horns, tail, and a chain. My brother and I were so frightened that we promised obedience and prayed to our guardian angel.

Music was my daily remedy. I either listened to some, or played some. Knowing the power of the sound and music, I hoped to be able to communicate to my Priest through my singing voice. OMBRA MAI FU from Handel's Xerxes became a means of communication. My heart and throat sang for my Priest. I also sang Bach's Ave Maria. Catholic archetypes never bothered me. The mind works with pictures and visualization. The universe works with sound. I nurtured my imagery and sent the waves of my own voice frequency to him, whom I loved.

The days were adding up. The children started school. Verne left for another trucking trip. We still avoided intimacy. I began to wonder whether he respected my wishes or if we were creating a gap between the two of us. I had to be truthful in my relationship.

Sometimes I felt sorry for my husband. He was kind, worked hard and seldom complained. I felt like betraying him. I had to make a choice. I chose my marriage. It was a reality of the time. We had a short honeymoon again, until I was kissed by true love. All this happened in the month of the Virgin, the maiden of the harvest.

The early morning of September 12th, 1988, I was kissed again by my husband on my right cheek. It was a loving ritual practised by him faithfully since we'd been together. He never woke me up in the mornings; he quietly got up and before leaving he gave me a kiss and wished me and the kids a great day. This morning was as usual. I woke up, scanned the room with my eyes and checked the clock. It was six in the morning. I had one hour left before the start of another busy day. I was trying to go back to sleep, but all of a sudden, I was standing on the cobble stone street, looking around to identify the location. There were people around me I could not see. I just felt their presence and heard them talking. The crowd spoke a different language - it sounded Germanic. The place was quite warm on this sunny day. There was a church at my far left and a few meters in front of me was a water canal with anchored small boats. Along both sides of the canal there was a lane of trees. The bridge at my left and at my right led to the other side of the canal, along which there was another pathway. All this time my eyes were focused on the houses attached to each other along the pathway across the canal. I could smell flowers from everywhere. I heard the sound of tramways, bicycle bells, and I could hear the boats' whistles in a nearby harbour. I could smell the sea! I was getting used to brightness and looked into a blue sky now. I saw a large white bird, whose wings spread about two meters wide, gliding across the sky at my right. He saw me! It was my Priest! I heard the crowd around me exclaiming in admiration "LOOK AT THAT BIRD!" He flew toward me and attempted to land. I was kissed by him on my right cheek! It was magical! Then he landed in front of me on the balancing beam made of the red oak tree trunk. The beam was carved by hand. Three seconds later, the bird descended off the beam and positioned himself on the opposite side of it. I was overwhelmed by his presence and extended my right arm to caress him. His soft white feathers felt warm! I touched his back and proceeded along the neck toward his head. His left eye looked into my eyes lovingly, radiating devotion. I must have pleased him with my touch, because he joyfully and rapidly rose over my head, forming a prolonged circle of his flight, directly into the blue sky. I lost the sight of him when he merged with the sun. I was blinded by its brightness. He appeared again and flew toward me, tracing an oval path. His colour had changed into a dark green now and his body became very thin. He kissed me again on my right cheek, showering me with love I had never known before. It was intimate and pure. When he completed the oval loop, he passed in front of my face, and changed again into a bird, looking like a phoenix this time, with emerald and indigo colours of his plumage. He opened two pairs of wings. I heard the crowd exclaiming in awe "LOOK AT THOSE COLOURS!" The bird ascended energetically into the blue sky. His wings merged together creating a ring around his body and he assumed the form of the Saturn. The joy I felt was ineffable. I was still standing on the street, feeling its stones beneath my feet. Where was I? I touched my right cheek, feeling vibrations of the kisses. I placed my hand where true love had kissed me.

I was in my bed again, ecstatic with joy. Where is my love? Does he live in those houses?

What a gift this was for my upcoming forty second birthday! I added another blessing to my life and thanked the Creator for everything that led to this moment.

There was no way that Hanna would not be notified about my experience. She asked me a few smart questions to make sure that my husband's kiss could not be mistaken with the bird's kiss. The difference was remarkable in intensity and chronology. We made guesses about the bird and the location. The closest we came to was a heron and any city in the Low Countries that had water canals. We thought of Amsterdam and Brugge, yet neither of us visited these cities. I just passed through Amsterdam once on the way from Schiphol airport to Centraal Station taking train to Paris.

I phoned Aaron about my "dream". He was very happy about it and implied that the bird represented nobility and that the set of double wings signified the flight of time through this three dimensional world. When I told him that I must find the exact location, or, I'd never have peace, he encouraged me only vaguely. He thought it wasn't necessary. For the first time I stopped trusting him. I felt that for some strange reason he was actually discouraging me and I could not understand his motivation. I knew he wanted me to work on my marriage. Aaron was a firm believer in the NOW. Whatever we have in our life at the given moment is there to teach us something, and we are to seek a perfect relationship in the present and with the present situation. He said that we have no relationship with anyone except ourselves and that we are only learning how to relate.

Aaron had a message for me. About one week later I decided to work on my marriage and create the dream I had prior to my wedding. It was about time to bring some realistic sense to my daily existence and create harmony and balance.

We were entering the sign of Libra, the sign of balance, and the month number eight. The energy flow within the figure eight is self regenerating, running on its own power. It also represents continuity and it is clearing and purifying.

PROMISE

ALL was back to normal. Every day had about the same routine. It felt comfortable. I put out the garden for the season, raked the leaves, cleaned the windows and waited for the winter with the longest night of the year.

Verne and I went to Octoberfest again where we met two years ago. We danced with each other the entire night. Being excessively attentive and cautious not to give him the slightest reason for jealousy and insecurity, all went well and we entwined again.

A couple of nights later, during an early morning hour, I was half awake, feeling the freshness of the wind. Our bedroom window was always slightly open. I thought the wind was coming through the window when, suddenly, in front of me I saw my Priest walking toward me with his arms reaching out. He wore an ankle-length dark tunic. The strong western wind blew against him; its force preventing him from reaching the shore where I stood. I noticed he walked on the stormy water. He called out to me "Promise me you will keep on searching for me! Promise that you'll find me! Promise!" I promised. I attempted to take him out of the water and onto the shore. I was extending my arms toward him, but I could not reach him. There was a distance between us. My heart was torn. I felt his desperation and his cry for help.

Nothing was the same in my marriage after this lucid dream. The honeymoon was over. That same day I took off my wedding band and placed it under a lamp on the night table next to our bed. Our bed was an antique bed and was not a king or queen size. It was a double bed.

I prayed for help and answers, and looked for literature that would help me identify what I was going through. There is a saying that life starts at forty-two. Where was my start, since all effect is the result of a cause? Then again, I was the creator of my present situation, the actor on the stage of my own life, trying to remember what the next line was. With all the tools I was given at the time of my conception, when every cell of mine was created to form a temple to house my spirit, those same tools had to assist me now. Within its matrix, there was encoded information for which I needed a key. I had been given a key to the Catholic University. Which door should I open? At times I hesitated to accept messages literally. There is more than one meaning to everything. As above, so is below. Somehow, I had to get to the next line of my comedy. It wasn't even funny anymore. But life consists of ups and downs. We soar to heights as an eagle, and between those high moments we creep in the lowest, hiding ourselves in the sands of the desert, crawling backward, just like scorpions.

Libra was over and the challenge of the Scorpio energy presented itself very clearly. The month number nine - the first power of three. It can either expand itself into the second power of eighty one, or consume itself. Was I anxious and pushing too hard to fly among eagles, perhaps? If we are at peace with ourselves, we can connect to the universal mind, which is omnipotent, omnipresent and omniscient.

I needed a dose of good humour to allow myself to recuperate from my seriousness. The quest of our Selves cannot afford heaviness. I've seen far too many serious spiritual seekers, the martyrs, judgemental toward anyone who dared to have some fun. I was going to challenge it. God must have a sense of humour! How could He otherwise create this universe with laughter in it?

Verne and I were going to go to the Halloween dance. We had to be original. I went to the thrift store and bought black satin pants that had a leather look, and a black top that suited the fabric. Verne had a black turtleneck and trousers. With some silver glitter chains, some red, and a few stars for our faces, we became Mister and Miss Universe. Everybody read us at the dance. I had on both sleeves in silver glitter written MISS UNIVERSE and on the back I broke it into MISS-UNI-VER-SE. Over my bosom, in the same silver, I had the MILKY WAY and right under my belly in the red glitter the BLACK HØLE, with the O crossed like a stop sign. And those who read my buttocks had more to laugh about. I placed on one half a silver Moon Crescent to moon the world and on the other half I placed an image of the BIG DIPPER, with its name included. My husband was a perfect match with MR. UNIVERSE on his sleeves and on his back, yet over his chest he had written in the same silver glitter OMNIPOTENT and from that point straight down into his groin area he wore a long tie that was getting wider toward the lowest point, with gradually enlarged letters saying EXPANDINK. The last four letters fitted right over the private area. We were nominated by most people as the best costumes.

The celebration of the night transformed itself at midnight to enter the All Soul's Day. Black and White are always in the company of each other. The balance was back. The challenge of the Scorpio is the transformation and transcendence.

Even Hanna noticed that I was more peaceful again. I allowed the natural flow to help me in my search. If I were to stay with Verne, it would happen so. Outwardly I was supportive of my marriage; inwardly I was seeking a deep spiritual union. I read somewhere that we love only one male through many men. Therefore, the ultimate relationship exists, but we must be ready for its manifestation. I had to prepare for the ultimate.

There was no answer from the Notre Dame School. I was in a stalemate. Some days it bothered me. Those days I sang Ombra Mai Fu again. In the middle of November another gift came my way.

Toward the morning I heard in my left ear a name repeated twice. A pleasant man's voice was giving me this name. It was very familiar and I felt that the first name resembled a Czech name Jarek, but it sounded more like Yariek. The surname had ended with "man" and the word "library" came through. I had perceived in my mind that the name came through a phone call. I stood in front of a Gothic arch shaped door and pressed a doorbell. A tall partially bald DOORMAN wearing a preacher's outfit opened the door. I said that Yariek wanted to speak with me. I heard a resonant man's voice coming from the left saying: "Tell her I'll speak with her when I am done!" The preacher told me that Yariek was very busy. Instead of being at the door entrance now, I was standing on the sandy path leading to the ascending stone stairway. The word SENDERO flashed in my mind.

I added this dream to my journal. I knew I was given another key and had to figure out its meaning. I remembered the energy of Yariek from one special experience I was awarded on Mother's Day in the year 1980, soon after I married Eduardo. At that time Yariek was an overseeing teacher, pleased with my progress. It happened in a location that actually exists, yet, my experience took place on the etheric plane. It was in a large cathedral dedicated to Mary. There was a grotto by its foundation. I remembered the exact interior, including paintings of angels and clouds on the high ceiling above the unusual altar that had a shape of a large desk. Where was it?

Before my father died, he took my brother and me to the puppet theatre occasionally and bought us a couple of puppets representing Father and Son. Their names were Spejbl and Hurvínek We played puppets and created a script right on the spot. I became a puppeteer and my submissive puppet did exactly what I expected. It surrendered to my guidance. I trusted the process of my quest and I surrendered. It was a conscious decision which created an irresistible impulse that guided me to look into a box with souvenirs from my European honeymoon. I ended up holding a pamphlet in my hand, which I picked up in the church of St. Germain-au-Près in Paris. The bronze eagle bible stand near the entrance inside this church made a powerful impression on me. There were many pamphlets in the church available. I picked only one about the pilgrimage to Lourdes. After reading it now, I looked up information about the location in the Encyclopaedia Britannica. It was the cathedral I visited in 1980! Was I to return to Europe and find answers there? We were entering Sagittarius - the Archer. My aim was my native continent for completion of number ten - December. Ten is number One and Zero. It is the beginning without the end.

ADAM AND EVE

DECEMBERS in my city can be either very cold, or quite pleasant. It depends on the direction of the wind. The daily transportation of the children to their schools and back, plus the care of Andrew, household, and the yard kept me very busy. I was looking forward to our first family Christmas with Verne.

The preparations can be exciting. We bought many beautiful decorations and chains and made a ritual of decorating the tree. I placed my favourites in the center. It was a dove and the Star of David. Some call it the Seal of Solomon.

Christmas music was played at all times in our home. Whenever I had a moment, I practiced singing for the Advent concert of the Bach Choir. The major part of the program was "Jesu Meine Freude", meaning "Jesus, my Joy". It is a very devotional piece.

Our concert went very well. Verne didn't show up. I noticed that he was not thrilled about my involvement with the choir. Verne was by birth Sagittarius, just like both my parents and my daughter Monica. I learned not to challenge any of them. It can result in a volcanic eruption. They are Fire. I was an Earth sign with Sagittarius ascendant at the time of my birth. I never was a typical Virgo.

This was the first time since my first marriage that I could plan Christmas shopping without worrying. It felt great! I was responsible with expenses, selecting practical gifts. Maria and Andrew still believed in Santa Claus, Jean made me believe that she did. Monica helped with gift wrapping and some Christmas baking. It looked like a perfect festive season on the outside. Inside, I was longing for the union with my beloved and hoped for some miracle, or a sign.

In the evenings, before I retired, I retreated into the living room by the Christmas tree, treating myself to the luxury of daydreaming, attaching wings to my thoughts. The blinking of colourful Christmas lights almost hypnotized me. I used the Star of David as a gateway, while listening to music by a Chilean composer Joakín Bello that my Chilean friends sent me for Christmas. I was again indulging in the piece called Andesenios. It starts with a water fountain introducing Tibetan music and blends into a Gregorian chant sung by well selected male voices, overlapped by angelic voices. The last lines of devotionally repeated "Gracia Criste" ended in electronic sounds with a soundtrack of birds and a puma.

In moments of devotion we become truly intimate with ourselves, when nothing else really matters. I can understand the subtle passion of the monk. Expressing love toward a human being is somehow different from the love we feel toward our Creator, unless we connect to the divine essence in the human being. Only then our love becomes divine and we revere all life. Once we taste the sweetness of that perfect love, we are willing to do anything to feel it again. For that love people made superhuman tasks and by their action left us a statement that life without true love is empty. Everyone seeks completion in union, whatever their consciousness is. Some express it in their promiscuous nature, some fight to conquer, others write and compose, some die for it. The Christ child within is the fruit of the perfect union of Alpha and Omega.

In my native Bohemia we celebrate the birth of the Christ child on the twenty fourth of December. It is the day of Adam and Eve, the day to celebrate their oneness before the Exile from the Garden of Eden, or, their return to Paradise. The Seal of Solomon, the Star of David, represents that perfect union.

Everyone was happy about the gifts they received for Christmas. Everyone, but Verne. He complimented on my smart shopping and the next day he asked me how I paid for it. I told him the truth. Some cash, some with credit card. When I took the children skiing during the school break, we had to return home. The credit card was cancelled. It explained why Verne didn't want to join us. We had an argument. My peace was taken from me. I grieved. Every year I was reminded that Christmas season is an intense time. It reminds us of who we are and what side of life we represent. Verne was on the opposite side of mine. I was not upset about it. I was going to grow faster next to him. We still shared the same bed, but made no love. He and I could not enter a dimension of Paradise together.

I became an observer of my own act in action. Obviously, this marriage was coming to completion. It was clear to me when Verne asked for a divorce. I wanted him to reconsider and to be less rational. We became a couple again just for a short while. It didn't feel right. There was no presence of devotion or love for the other. Yet, I was grateful that he was in my life. He assisted me in meeting my beloved and helped me with the children for a while. I couldn't help the feeling that he completed something he owed me from the past. Aaron did a reading for us when Verne and I were dating. He said it himself that our relationship was strictly karmic. Without Verne's help I wouldn't be able to travel to Santiago and be generous with my friends. Verne held a very special post in my life. Now, he was willing to step down and allow me the freedom to find my path to Eden to complete the cycle and partake of the Fruit of the Tree of Life and share it with my Adam.

PRAYER OF THE VIRGIN

DOUBTLESSLY, there was an intense time ahead. I began to depend on my strength, patience and other virtues. Every day introduced another surprise. The festive season was over and we parted with our Christmas tree. I placed the Star of David into a separate box with other special objects that were meaningful to me. Among them was a Rosary Eduardo gave me for Christmas in 1981 in Chile. I took out a note with Love Rosary and found comfort in the prayer, running beads between my fingers. It became my daily ritual before falling asleep.

Exactly on the last day of January 1989, I was taken from the prayer into a room that had three objects on the wall, all of them made of glazed ceramic, except the one in the middle. The object on the left side was in the shape of a three story brown house with a word ANTWERPEN over the large ribbon at its base. The middle object was an oval mirror in a golden frame. On the right side there was a brown cross with a male figure hanging upside down – the Hangman. I could smell a fragrance, but could not recognize its source. The walls in the room were of peach colour. I wrote about the experience in my journal. It was a message indicating that I had my answers in Belgium in Antwerp.

I sent a letter to my friends in Santiago, asking them to speak with the director of the Notre Dame School about my request for Father Jacob's address. At this time schools had summer holidays. I had to wait for my answer for other six weeks.

Ray phoned me about a dream he had. He said that my Priest was in turmoil not knowing how to find me. He also said that I had a better chance of finding him. This information placed more responsibility on me, and I ached again. My prayers to the Divine Mother became a daily necessity. At this time I needed more than fortitude. I asked for a direction to the next step.

Within one week another important dream came through. I was walking in a European city on the narrow sidewalk, looking at numbers of houses. All these houses were attached to each other. One entrance door was open. I entered and sat down in a waiting room furnished with antiques arranged in a cozy way. I observed wall hangings. Paintings were of Flemish landscapes. I could see into the next room through a glass door covered with a fine lace curtain. There were two men in conversation. After the blond man left, the other tall man asked me in. He knew my name. He wore a black tunic. I was asked to sit at his desk and he shifted his chair close to mine. He was about my age, dark hair, very handsome features. Our eyes delighted in reciprocity. It was extremely loving and sweet. His blue eyes were deep and pure. Everything about him was very spiritual. He passed me a white envelope in which I found a vial with a white powder and a hand written note saying that I was to use the substance of alchemy. The note was signed by the writer. He is known as the ALCHEMIST. I cannot reveal his name. I was filled with gratitude. My friend nodded in agreement with the note. Then he showed me to the door. The blond friend, whose name was Josef, just came back. Out of the door, into a street and ....I was back in my bed.

I couldn't recognize the city where I was, yet, the personality was someone very familiar to me. In time, it would be revealed.

In March, I received a phone call from Santiago. My friends had the address of Father Jacob. They dictated it to me. It was a parish in Deurne, in Belgium. I chose a post card with the beautiful Lake Louise and wrote to Father Jacob that I had a story to tell him and also that I had the key to Iannua Coeli. I included my address and mailed it on the same day.

GOOD NEWS

THERE was a tension in our home in the evenings. Verne kept more to himself and spent less time with the children. Our double bed became a single bed overnight - I began to sleep on the sofa in the living room. Verne stopped talking about a divorce when I told him that I would not oppose it if he petitioned. He didn't come to Monica's graduation either. Everything was just a matter of time.

In the beginning of May, a Petition for a Divorce was served to me and I had to learn in a hurry how to answer it on my own. I could not afford a lawyer. Clerks in the court house were helpful with guidance. I had nothing to ask of the marriage, no child maintenance was involved. Our case was simple. The children were calm because I was calm. There was no animosity. They liked Verne, but he was in their life for a too short time. Monica was concerned about our survival. She was graduating from high school and wanted to go to a Bible College in Swift Current in Saskatchewan. I would rather have her in the city studying for a practical career. She had already decided. Luckily, she was offered a loan that she accepted. She encouraged me about my possible future work, suggesting interpreting, translating, marketing, sewing, and babysitting. Yes, there were many decisions to be made.

At all times my mind had to be clear and calm. I had to find a way into the future, willing to consider all opportunities. A few days after I was served a petition, I received a short letter from Father Jacob from Belgium. He was very curious how I knew about him and expressed a desire to hear about the story I had for him. He answered me in Spanish, but mentioned that he was also French speaking. He moved from the parish in Deurne four years ago, yet, my card was forwarded to him. He resided in Antwerp now. My hopes were high!

I phoned Hanna immediately and she was very excited about it. We talked like a two teenage girls, fantasizing all the possible outcomes. Ray was informed as well, except he was not too happy about it. It really surprised me.

I answered Jacob's letter within a couple of days. I was very particular about proper spelling. This letter was in Spanish. I briefly described the encounter and mentioned how I found out about him from Eduardo, his former student. The answer came in twenty two days. Jacob was not the man I saw, but he was so curious about my search, that he offered friendship and possible assistance in my quest.

I felt grateful and also a bit disappointed. Obviously, Antwerp had some other offerings for me. Naturally, I planned on visiting the city whenever possible, but at the same time, I hoped for some kind of message that would lead me to my beloved Priest. I kept on asking my Divine Mother.

On the night of twenty first to twenty second of June 1989, the shortest night of the year, I prayed Love Rosary, as usual. I could feel a gentle freezing sensation coming from my feet toward my face. All of a sudden, a current of wind, like a vortex, took me out of my body into the unknown space. Instantly, I was placed in a room with bookshelves, desks and chairs. It looked like a library. There I saw my beloved Priest standing, conversing with some other man of his height. They both noticed me and stopped talking, looking at me. Rapidly swirling toward my beloved, I reached with my right hand to touch his left arm. I felt warm flesh. He wore a safari type outfit, with a short sleeve shirt and slacks. The contact of my touch had powered the vortex to draw me rapidly away from him and I found myself floating, being surrounded by many masks of light electric blue colour, introducing themselves to me one by one. After maybe ten of them,

I was back in my body again, trying to feel the toes first. It wasn't coming easily. I was holding the beads between my fingers. Would repetition and mantra of Love Rosary be this effective? What was the message behind this event? Am I to look for him in the library? This was by far the most intimate contact we've had. Interestingly, we were entering the sign of our encounter - Cancer.

How much destiny was there involved in my experience, or how much desire had created the result? When we ask, we shall receive and we do receive. Is it right to ask? How can we possibly have the wisdom of knowing what's the best for us?

I began to include the Lord's Prayer. It is more submissive and I truly wanted that which I deserved and was ready for. There was another gift sent to me. It was again audible and had a very specific instruction about my personal spiritual direction. Neither can this one be shared. It empowered me tremendously and confirmed to me that I was doing the right thing by focusing on my inner spirituality.

The summer was challenging. Verne moved out, took my car under pretence of taking it for a service and oil change, and I had to manage with available resources. Our vegetable garden helped us to survive. I had to hire an inexpensive lawyer who would help me to retrieve my car. She figured I had rights to ask for a half of Verne's estate. We didn't have a prenuptial agreement. I agreed to ask for a half of equity gained for duration of our marriage. After I received half of the settlement, paid the lawyer and insured my car again, an eviction notice written by Verne's lawyer was served. I asked to stay in the house until it sold, to gain time needed to find something affordable. I turned to subsidized housing for help, but their waiting list was too long. A small financial settlement supported us for three more months. I was resourceful enough to stretch it up to Christmas. Worrying solves nothing. I had to focus on positive aspects of life to keep my sanity.

On the last week of summer vacation I went to a social gathering where the invited speakers introduce a forthcoming seminar or promote some kind of teaching. This time the invited speaker talked about Hermetism. Ray came along with me. The night before going to the lecture, I felt an inner excitement and it intensified in the lecture room. I looked around. Among familiar faces I observed few newcomers, but my eyes were fixed on the Germanic face of a young man in his late thirties, who was absorbed in the presentation. When the lecture was over, one of the friends insisted I must meet Marc. He introduced me to that young man.

Marc just came from Belgium. I asked him if he was from Antwerp, but he said that he was from Gent. We liked each other. He was a distributor of a very unusual product called Vitaflorum. I asked him to come to my place and tell me more about it. He wrote down my phone number.

Ray looked at me from the corner of his eye.

"Ingrid, you might have met your contact! How is your gut doing now?"

"Ray, do you realize how close Gent is to Antwerp? Marc speaks excellent English. He must have some promising connections there! Why would he show up in this lecture? How many people are interested in Hermetism, really?"

I was ecstatic and more so when I thought of Marc.

He came in the afternoon. He and his family had moved to Canada just a month ago in hope of creating a better future for their four children. Marc came from Gent, but he grew up in Antwerp and lived there until recently. He knew many people in that city who were involved in a personal and spiritual growth. When I described my beloved Priest, his mind went blank. Later on during the visit, he spoke of his school teacher, whose name was Josef. He was a priest. His features were similar to my beloved's. Marc's mother was a teacher in the same school. Marc promised that he'd find out more from his mother.

Within a month, I had Josef's phone number. Marc warned me that Josef was married and had children now. He obviously had left Church. It was fine with me.

One late night I gathered courage to dial Josef's number. He answered. I asked him if he was in Santiago de Chile on that particular day or knew of someone from his ranks who travels there occasionally. Josef asked me why I was looking for that person. He already knew that Marc gave me his number. I told him it was personal and that I could explain more in the letter. He gave me his address and insisted that I must write him about it soon and that he'd answer.

When I hung up the phone, I was soaked in my own perspiration. His beautiful tenor voice still resonated in my ears. He must have been a great chanter! I tried to attach Josef's voice to my beloved's body. It fitted perfectly!

I bought a very special writing paper with matching envelopes and scented it with rose fragrance. The letter was written in calligraphy and mailed by registered mail.

Meanwhile, I began to plan a trip to Europe. Logically, it was an impossible dream. I was at the end of my resources, had nothing to sell, no part-time job I could take on, except some babysitting, and had four children to feed. Neither did I know my future address. But I had faith, I had love, I had hope. I had it all!

I chose to fight the eviction in the court. The Subsidized Housing Cooperative did not have any unit available for us yet. The judge didn't give me any chance to speak on my behalf. Verne's lawyer was quick to speak and I didn't know when there was a right time to say something. A decision was made: a court order for an eviction for mid November. I had one week to find a place with the little money left from the settlement. I told the judge that he made a decision without hearing my story. He heard me out, but stated that a made decision cannot be changed, but, they would discuss my case in Chambers. I couldn't believe the injustice and wondered how many poor people lose their case because they cannot afford a lawyer. And on top of that, I had to call the judge "Mi Lord"! I broke down. In tears, I went to the office of the housing cooperative. They must have taken pity on me, because the receptionist gave me an address of a four bedroom unit that would be available right after Christmas. I reserved the unit with a small down payment.

I phoned Verne's lawyer and told him about my move after Christmas. He said that I could not go against a court order and that we would be thrown out on the street, regardless of the weather. I didn't believe him. I inquired other places about this law. The lawyer was right. I phoned Verne. I hadn't spoken with him since our separation. He was reluctant about giving us an extension. He wanted to sell his house quickly. I had to go deeply into his conscience. Then, he agreed. It had to pass another court hearing, but it became legal. Only after moving out was I entitled to another small financial settlement that would support us for four more months. Marc helped me in the meanwhile with a small loan.

This winter was too cold. In my heart I had warmth. Letters from Christian and Jacob kept on coming regularly and I answered them within a few days. Whenever I had a spare moment, I taped some Christmas music with carols I sang myself. These were Christmas gifts for friends I loved. Twice a week, I went for rehearsals for our upcoming concerts.

In December I was astonished by the news: General Pinochet stepped down to give way to a more democratic leadership in Chile. Around that time the Berlin wall was taken down. Synchronicity? That would be impossible to sell to me. Someone is playing the Almighty. I chose to skip the three capital letters that came to my mind. Obviously, events are premeditated. I stopped trusting history again. Some say that history is written in the stones of the Great Pyramid. Nostradamus prophesied many events, but at the end of his life he stated that we have the power to change the future. I believed in that power.

I decided to remain positive and give power to the forces of Light that will lead humanity into Peace. I made a promise to myself that the following summer I will visit Europe and my native land. When I left Bohemia, I never hoped to be able to return. The military communist system was there to stay for a long time. Now they talked about a democratic election and a candidate who was a prominent prisoner for many years, a writer with suspiciously short pants, which had to be noticed by everyone. They shrunk during his visit to the United States.

When we are in the middle of chaos, we lose sight and understanding. We become confusion itself. Only an outsider can see clearly what's going on. The same thing was happening with my search. At times, when I was too absorbed in my desire to find my beloved soon, I was losing clarity.

Marc was going to visit his family in Belgium for New Year. He asked me to come along and meet Josef. It was not financially feasible for me. Marc was going to visit him and perhaps bring me the answer. Still, he helped me with moving prior to his leaving.

We had a humble Christmas, but were not depending on anyone. I invested a part of my little settlement into a line of products that was very sellable and could support us. I became an entrepreneur of the nineties, not knowing where the next meal was coming from, but positive and doing the best every day.

Anxiously, I'd been waiting for Marc's call from Belgium. He phoned me after his return. Josef told him that my letter was already answered. Waiting for it every day became exciting - I might receive the good news after all!

ANSWERED PRAYER

ON some days I was getting a response from potential customers. Some people offered to organize a home show. Sometimes I made some money, but mostly I had to invest it back into buying a new product. Not many multilevel marketing companies allow freedom. Many put conditions. Mine did. It became a struggle. Despite my faith, I worried. Fortunately, I could sew. I made myself a classy wardrobe from remnants that cost almost nothing. I had to look presentable. The way to success is long and it takes many hours of work without pay. Some days I felt discouraged. I spent hours on the phone, and generated hardly any business. I became stressed and began to feel it in my body. Fatigue became a burden of my daily life. We couldn't eat properly anymore - most of our meals were prepared from potatoes, legumes and included bread that I made. If I didn't have Hanna to talk to, I would have had much tougher times in dealing with crisis. She always said that I was a survivor and made good things happen.

"Ask!" she said. "Why don't you ask for more business?"

She felt that I was not assertive enough in my prayers. That was a new attitude for me. The truth is that I never knew how to ask for myself. I did it for everyone else, but myself. Why not try? My friends Jacob and Christian were praying for me, as they claimed. Why couldn't I? I wrote down what I needed: just enough money to provide for my children, to get to Europe and back and for current expenses for my family while I would be gone. My prayer was spoken and visualized in detail, with added emotions. After the ritual, I slept very peacefully. I decided not to worry anymore and to surrender completely.

The following week became very busy. I had a show with good sales almost every night and more shows were booked. The airline was paid for the ticket. Other shows provided funds for other expenses.

Before the end of May I was flying home to Europe. I didn't have to worry about lodging either. Jacob had a place for me in Antwerp and the rest would be provided by the Universe. Once I get home to Bohemia, I could stay with some of my friends and relatives, who would, hopefully, recognize and remember me. I had no time to notify anyone except Jacob by phone. So far, I had no answer from Josef. I assumed that the letter got lost. The same phenomenon happened a few years ago with letters to Rosa's family. None arrived. Obviously, I was supposed to travel there personally and check things out on my own.

Just a couple of days prior to my departure to Europe, a friend, who was at some conference in Montreal, brought me a cassette tape to listen to. It was entitled "The Future Self". It explained the nineties and late eighties in terms of changes that are due to cosmic energy causing our glandular system to respond. In some bodies the changes will be less favourable, in others very positive. It all depended on the attitude of the mind and the body's readiness for changes. Diet and cleansing were highly stressed. Intuition would be the language of the future. The woman speaker talked about an incredible acceleration of events and of the coming together of science, art, and philosophy. Based on our commitment in daily practice, we can actively participate in the outcomes. Every change can be manifested on our plane of existence when our minds allow it to actualize itself. Our mind is the doorway and we have the power to make things happen. In other words, the Creator is powerless without our permission to act.

Wow! It was powerful! I was ecstatic about this information and felt absolutely comfortable about the specified requests in my prayers. Again, I was reminded how important each of us is in the vast Universe. This realization was my armour for the trip. I just knew that this trip would make a difference in mine and other people's lives.

ANTWERPEN

DIRECTLY from Amsterdam, I went by train to Antwerp, enjoying the site of typical Dutch apartments with windows dressed in white lacy curtains. Toward the Belgian border the style changed. There is a marked difference between the styles of the two countries.

Travelling by train is very much like travelling in life. Places and people come your way when you are there in the right time and space. All you have to do is to be there and observe what's going on. It is much better to be awake or, the opportunity to experience something particular will never come back again. At the crossroads there is more activity. Direction signs, people waiting or running, some loaded with heavy luggage, some travel lightly. Again, I was reminded of the illusion of being in motion when the train on the parallel rail starts to move and you actually believe that yours is moving. There is always a feeling of fear associated with it. Fear of leaving too soon, not being ready for a departure, or leaving without the party you're travelling with. I remembered this fear from my childhood, when I was travelling by train with my mother. It happened at the crossroads with a longer stop, when she went to get me a lemonade, leaving me by the window so I could see her. Another train came by and I lost the sight of her. I was afraid that she would board the other train instead. Then the train moved and I feared that my mother was left behind. Only after a while, when the other train was gone and I realized that we were still waiting, I felt safe again. At the crossroads it is better to look ahead.

Before long, two hours passed and the train was arriving at Antwerpen Centraal. I was instructed to get off at Berchem, the next stop. Jacob was either to meet me there, or, I was to phone him. I had to phone. He gave me the address to get to by taxi. It was just three blocks away. It was the home of his parents. They were the sweetest old people I've met in a long time. Jacob was on his way.

Even though I had a photograph of Jacob, I couldn't imagine him the way he was. He came with a sincere smile and lit up face. He gave me a brotherly kiss and bubbled words of welcome both in Spanish and French, so his parents could participate. Obviously, they must have known something about me from Jacob.

That same afternoon he took me to Deurne and showed me a parish to which I sent my card. Now Jacob worked as a chaplain in the institute for handicapped in Brecht, where he was much happier. He liked to work with children.

Later on, he drove me to a park that was very special to him. It is called Boeckenberg, meaning the 'Book Mountain'. It was his favourite place ever since his childhood. He learned how to swim in the local swimming pool.

We walked on the pathway slowly, getting used to each other's accents. The aged tall trees witnessed the conversation of the two people who had a lot in common. We both loved children, were devotional in a healthy way, loved outdoors and classical music.

Jacob asked me what my plans were and I told him that I thought of visiting Lourdes and going home to Bohemia for three weeks. He was happy to hear about Lourdes.

"Sister, you wrote me once that you would like to be baptized by immersion and asked me if I could baptize you. You don't need me for that! I am just a simple priest. In Lourdes you can be baptized in holy water! Nobody will ask you any question. Baptism is for everyone, just like the Sun shines for everyone! Nobody asked me any questions there either. When I was immersed in that water, I felt like a million dollar man and could hardly feel the cold water. You're going to Lourdes for your baptism, Sister!"

"Actually, Jacob, I am going there for other reason. I must see the church's interior and I will probably meet someone interesting there."

"Do not tell me, Sister that you hope to find your man there! He is not a priest! The one you are looking for is more special. Seek and you shall find!"

We came to a bridge that connected both banks of a large man made pond. Jacob became silent for a while. He pointed at the crest carved into a stone railing and showed me the Latin words engraved into it.

"This message is for you, Ingrid: NEC FALLERE, NEC FALLI."

"What does it mean, Jacob?"

"DO NOT DECEIVE, DO NOT BE DECEIVED. Ingrid, you are looking for love believing that the man you saw on the street of Santiago can return your love to you. What if he cannot? There may be another reason for your quest, Sister! Remember, our heart is not quiet until it finds what it is looking for. You are not looking for that man! You are looking for love because you already know of such love. Ingrid, there are other men who can offer you that love. Why don't you settle with someone nice, create a family again. Why do you believe that the man you're looking for is the only one who deserves you?"

"I promised him that I'd find him! He wants me to!"

"How can anyone ask of you so much? You travel half the Earth, spend money you don't have, make sacrifices!"

"Jacob, I love him! I cannot be involved with anyone else. It is not possible for me. Even if I tried, I can't!"

"Well, Sister, you must know something I don't know. I became a priest while very young. I never loved a woman."

"Do you regret it?"

"No, I do not. My mission is in my work. Besides, if I were married, who would take you places in Antwerpen and take you for a Belgian beer? Come, Sister, over there is a nice quiet restaurant. We can have something to eat and toast with beer. I thirst! I thirst for truth, wisdom, and beer. But, before we leave this bridge, I want to show you a secret door."

Jacob led me to an old wooden door of some shelter or underground storage.

"Here the most important writings were stored during the war. There is always a patron who looks after our knowledge!"

"Who were the patrons here, Jacob?"

"The Counts of Boeckenberg."

"Was that their crest?"

"Yes, it is their crest, Sister. Now, come, I am thirsty!"

Jacob offered me his arm and led me toward the restaurant in the middle of the woods. We were the only guests there. In our conversation we talked about my children, Eduardo and Jacob's years in Chile. Then we planned for the following day after he'd serve the morning mass in the Institute's church. Jacob was going to show me real Antwerpen, with Rubens' works, statue of ogre and the largest gothic cathedral of Belgium, dedicated to Our Lady. I enjoyed every moment with Jacob, who physically was an attractive Flemish type, but looked nothing like my beloved.

When we returned to his parents' home, he showed me a room I would use. It used to be his bedroom, but for many years now he has resided in places of his work. After a long trip and a busy day, I slept extremely well.

ALCHEMIST

THE early morning airplanes woke me up, but I already had my seven-hour sleep. Later on I found out from Jacob's mother that we were near the Deurne International Airport. I had some time to myself. I was anxiously waiting for a later hour to phone Josef. In the meantime, I wrote in my Journal about all that had transpired. I described Jacob in one long paragraph. He had the title of a "Brother" whom I've known before we had met. I forgot to ask him about the meaning of his name. Jacob is James; the Spanish call James either Jaime or Santiago. I made a connection to Jacob through Santiago. His surname is De Schryver. What does that mean? I contemplated all the messages I received in the outer world: Boeckenberg, the secret door to knowledge, the crest with a LION, and the powerful words.

Toward eight o'clock I dialled Josef's number. A woman's voice told me that he only comes for weekends. He was working in Holland. I had three days left to wait.

After a lovely continental breakfast and Mme De Schryver's constant talking, Jacob came over to pick me up. I appreciated the French spoken in their family. Madame was my number one teacher. She introduced me to television news, excited about an upcoming democratic election in Czechoslovakia. She thought it was unusual to have a writer for a candidate. Then she said that their family name means THE WRITER.

Tramway number thirteen took us to the Green Square, where the famous statue of Peter Paul Rubens and an overpowering nearby tower of the Cathedral of Our Lady are. The charming cobble stone street lined with outdoor coffee shops guided us to the main door of the cathedral.

Having a passion for forms in art, I spent most of the time in front of huge Flemish paintings and statues of Peter and Paul, which guarded the main corridor. Peter held two keys in his hand. I pointed it out to Jacob and asked if he knew why he had two keys to Heaven. Jacob had an immediate answer.

"One key is made of gold. It opens the door of male energy, the Son in the outer world. The other key is made of silver that opens the door of female energy. Like Sun and Moon."

"Where did you get this explanation, Jacob? Catholics didn't teach you this! Do you actually know what you are talking about?"

"I figured that wisdom is hard to obtain, so I read. I read it somewhere."

In a soft voice, to preserve a quiet atmosphere, I collaborated,

"Sun and Moon are used in Alchemy as symbols of balance between male and female energy and also of the outer manifestation of the inner creation. The lunar way is the inner way to enlightenment. The solar way is the external way. Both should be balanced and reflecting each other, just like the moonlight reflects the sunlight. It is the way of presenting the microcosmic reflection of the macrocosm. Some say that Peter represented the inner sexuality, which ultimately leads to spirituality. Peter also represented the corner stone of the Church. Therefore, the keys represent the balance within us to open the door to Kingdom of Heaven - the Iannua Coeli."

Jacob made no comment. I probably shouldn't have mentioned sexuality. People have a hang up over the word, thinking only in terms of genitals and intercourse. We proceeded further into the cathedral. Jacob took some time for himself, kneeling in front of a sculpture of Mary with the child. They both had Royal robes and a Crown. By its side I saw incredible wood carvings of apostles. My attention was focused on St. John, holding a Chalice. His face was refined and very feminine. The artwork in the cathedral was truly a treasure. I decided to come back. We had many other places to see.

From the Steen that was guarded by an ogre by the entrance, overseeing the nearby port on Schelde river, we went back toward the cathedral, passing by the City Hall and another sculpted formation dealing with the conflict between humans and giants. Soon we were on another street full of shops. Jacob stopped by one of them:

"Ingrid, I come here to buy books once in a while. Come in! You will like it."

I looked up to read the sign above the door. It was DEN ALCHEMIST. The Alchemist!

I was inside the store instantly. As soon as the lady clerk was free, I faced her with a question,

"I was supposed to meet someone here. He is a very spiritual man, tall, handsome, in his forties."

She passed me a business card saying,

"Then you should talk to Mr. Jan Snijder. He is such a man."

I read the card. Jan was an astrologer and psychologist. He lived on Golden Flea Street! The lady clerk observed me. I turned to her with another question:

"What street are we on? What is your address?"

"We are on STEENHOUWERSVEST, the Free Masons Street. But it relates to those having a breast plate."

She smiled very kindly at me. A sisterly soul! Buzzing was the right identification of my emotions. I was on the right track! Jacob observed us and perceived that something good was happening. I told the lady that I'll be back yet. She was easy to talk to. Her English was impeccable.

Jacob looked over my shoulder to read the card.

"Guldenvliestraat... that's in Berchem! The tram goes by. It is one street from Osylei, just three blocks from my parents' house. Do you want to take a tram there?"

"It would be faster, wouldn't it? Let's go, Jacob, something is beginning to happen in Antwerpen after all!"

Like two happy kids we strode quickly back to Green Square to get on our tramway. The number thirteen was just arriving.

Europe is so condensed. When you take public transportation and get to your destination in no time, you wonder why you didn't walk. From the tram stop we crossed one corner and appeared on a steep narrow sidewalk of Guldenvliestraat. We checked the numbers. Indeed, Jan's name was on the door bell. Jacob prevented me from ringing it:

"Sister, they must be having lunch now. My mother has a lunch ready for us. Let us go there first and then you can visit with Jan. You know your way now."

I agreed. Two hours later, I was back in the same location. I pressed the doorbell. The door was opened by a handsome tall man with dark hair and blue eyes. I was speechless for a moment. He was the man from my dream who passed me the envelope with a note and an alchemical substance!

*"Je voudrais parler avec vous, Monsieur. Est-ce que vous avez un moment?"**

He just kept on looking at me with gentle gladness and total acceptance of a surprising visit.

*"Oui, mais je ne parle pas Français,"*** he apologized.

*"Et moi, je ne parle pas Flamand! Quelle langue parlez-vous?"****

"English!" he said with hesitation, as if he hoped I'd speak the same language.

"Me too! Oh, what a relief!" I said while exhaling. I must have held my breath again. "My name is Ingrid Heller. I come from Canada. I must speak with you."

He invited me in and asked me to wait a moment as he had to finish his lunch in a hurry. He opened a door into a room with a chair to sit on and with some antique furniture.

With the exception of wall hangings, it looked like a mirror image of the room in the dream I had. The street and the houses of the dream looked almost identical.

* * * * * * * *

"I'd like to speak with you, Sir. Do you have a moment?"
"Yes, I do, but, I don't speak French."
"And I don't speak Flemish. What language do you speak?"

I observed a poster of the chart of The Cabbalistic Tree of Life, the map to inner Journey and understanding of life cycles. Three minutes later, Jan opened the glass door to his office and asked me to have a seat by his desk.

"What can I do for you, Ingrid?"

"I was instructed to come to Antwerp. I am looking for a man...."

"That should be easy to find. I suppose you are looking for a special man."

"Exactly! He is in his forties, is tall, handsome, noble looking, and is very spiritual. He also writes. I believe I am to find him in this city."

Jan is looking at a fixed point, rubbing his chin, thinking.

"Why Antwerpen?"

"He is either here or someone from Antwerp is to show me the way to him."

"It could be me who you are looking for. I am forty-two!"

"I already met him. I know what he looks like."

"If you met him, why do you look for him here?"

"We just saw each other in a real geographical place. We both were visitors there. We also parted from each other without any introduction."

"A typical meeting of the twins! They meet at the crossroads and inspire the highest in each other. You are doing the right thing. Keep on asking at the gates!"

"The Song of Solomon!" I exclaimed. "That is what's going on! Do you happen to know anyone of those special qualities here by the name of Josef?"

"In Holland, yes, but not here. I think you should be looking in Holland. There are some like that..."

He paused for a moment. I thought he searched in his memory bank for my man, so, I kept quiet.

"You know, Ingrid, you are very lucky to be at that point of uniting with your beloved. We truly earn it. The Divine Romance is for Divine Lovers. Your name was well chosen for you too: INGRID... you have INRI within your name. Igni Naturae

Renovatus Integra. By fire all nature is renewed. Fire of Spirit and Love is that powerful."

The door bell rang. Jan rose from his chair.

"My client is here. Is there a phone number where I could reach you? If something comes up, I will phone you!" he said, leading me to the door.

I phoned him and gave him a contact number in Antwerp from Jacob's home. Once more Jan encouraged me not to give up and keep on searching.

The rest of the afternoon Jacob and I passed in the Middelheim park, an outdoor museum with the most interesting sculptures. Some were fascinating. We took several pictures. One of them with a setting of a nobleman, sitting comfortably by the table, on which there was a book and menorah. I sat on his lap to pose for a picture. Jacob teased me that I found my man. We called my new immortal friend a DUKE. He had that appearance.

The outdoor restaurant at the park saved the thirsty Jacob again and I gladly joined him in a ritual of appreciating the Belgian beer. Wherever we went, there were all kinds of birds. Jacob explained that Belgium is rich in fauna. I asked him about herons. He told me that by the Dutch border in Berendrecht there is the largest blue heron colony in Western Europe. He offered to take me to Reigersbos in two days.

The next day I had entirely to myself. Jacob had to work. I went again to Den Alchemist with an intention of collecting more information. By the door I noticed a shelf full of flyers. I picked two of them that appealed to me.

On the way back I visited the cathedral again. Next to the main corridor was a chapel where people found some privacy for prayers. When everyone left, I went to read from the open Bible on the stand by the altar. The red ribbon bookmark kept the book open to one page. Interestingly, the text was about Mary Magdalene and her status of Virgin. Just like most of churches of Our Lady in France are dedicated to Mary Magdalene, so was this one. It goes together with French speaking nations. This Bible was in French. The royal robe and the crown therefore belonged to Mary Magdalene! Dukes of Brabant used to be rulers of what we presently call Belgium. They must have sponsored construction of many temples.

Walking back to Berchem, I enjoyed the atmosphere of this charming old city. The corner houses displayed a sculpture of the royal image of Mary and the Christ child in the niche on the second floor. It probably reflected the wealth of the landlord.

I phoned a number from one brochure I picked. This group made street presentations, acting a play that was intended to attract people interested in the spiritual growth. In Europe everything is hidden, secretive, hermetically sealed. It must be in European genes since the time of the inquisition. I was invited to meet the group. I went that same afternoon. They were lively, friendly, and happy people. I described my beloved and asked whether there is someone like him in Antwerp. They sent me to Nico Thelman's house.

On the way there, I stopped by the Rubens House. It was another treasure. I loved the garden with statues of Minerva and Mercury and its park-like landscape. Rubens, I heard, was a brilliant man. While painting, he carried on an intellectual or philosophical discussion and at the same time was dictating a letter to someone. He lived in Love.

Nico received me. He was tall, handsome, and had Flemish features in him. He carried himself with grace. He introduced me to Key Monebo, who was known for tours called "Esoteric Antwerp". Later on, it was sponsored by the municipality and she added other tours, taking people to museums, churches, and streets. Antwerp is full of symbols. It is like a book to read, if one knows how to read it.

Nico felt I should get in touch with Jan Snijder who knows just about anybody on the Path. People come to him for counsel, readings, guidance. Nico also felt that I might be able to find that person in Holland. He actually named a library where I could find some answers. He gave me the library's address and phone number, insisting that I must call first to make a reservation. It was a private library. I became very curious about the founder. His name was Mr. Ritman. He spent his airline catering company's profits on purchasing precious manuscripts, had them transcribed and translated into major languages, then published the limited editions of them all. I was in awe and blessed Mr. Ritman's work.

Nico was an interesting man. On his white moon crescent shaped desk a sculpture of Merlin holding a crystal ball attracted my attention. I BELIEVE IN MAGIC poster on the wall in the background promoted Nico's services. He was a magician of the 21st century and an illusionist. Since his childhood, his life experiences guided him to contemplate nature's laws, consciousness and the sacred psychology. He said that Jan Snijder understands these laws as well and that he was a true psychologist, just like Carl Jung was.

I wished I could have stayed at Nico's place longer, but I had to return to De Schryver's home on time, as I promised. Nico insisted I must keep in touch and definitely, must visit Ritman's Library.

In the late evening, after a beautiful supper and conversation with Jacob's parents, I retired. I added another day to my Journal. The day was magical. Nico's name was recorded as The El Man.

HERON

IT took less than one hour to get to Berendrecht by car. It was a small organized town. Jacob parked his car by the gateway of Reigersbos, the heron sanctuary. There was a restaurant by the park's gate. We walked into a park set in natural surroundings. It almost looked neglected. After a short walk, a very special house appeared in front of us that must have belonged to someone of noble background. We continued on the path, avoiding damp areas.

Jacob stopped to chat with a landscaper for a while, who cut the tall grass. They spoke in Flemish. I was able to I pick up some words - many came from German and with little imagination, I understood the rest of it. They talked about the man who lived in that white mansion. I could hardly imagine why anyone of privileged background would want to live in this wild and humid environment, unless they were patrons. The vision of my experience with a heron in the Low Countries city came back to my mind instantly. My beloved assumed the form of the bird in my lucid dream. I had to ask.

"Jacob, who lives in that white mansion?"

"A very well known gentleman. He is the president of the International Olympic Games Committee. He speaks several languages. He is a Count."

"Is he tall, attractive?" I asked anxiously.

"No, he is short."

I thought that Jacob was teasing me again.

"Oh, sure. He is short! How do you know, Jacob?"

"I've met him, Ingrid. He is short and older than the man you're looking for."

I was a bit disappointed. Why? If I had no expectations, I would be totally content and grateful for being able to see rare birds in their natural habitat, watch their flight from one tree to the other, checking on nests and feeding their young.

Jacob kept on observing me, smiling.

"Ingrid, you are just at the beginning of your quest. Relax, take it easy, enjoy! When you least expect it, what you're looking for will appear. Let go of expectations!"

Jacob was right. Aaron said the same thing to me. "Let go, set the man free!"

I had to pose by the park sign for another shot of Jacob's camera. I knew exactly what the next step was: the restaurant. Jacob had a blessed appetite, for his mother was an excellent cook. She was an alchemist in the kitchen. All of the food she prepared was permeated by her love.

We sat by the window and ordered our meal. I needed to get my mind off previous emotions. Luckily, Jacob asked me how my day went yesterday. This was my opportunity to talk about the chapter in the Bible inside the Cathedral.

"Did you know, Jacob, that the Cathedral in Antwerpen is dedicated to Mary Magdalene? Not at all to Jesus' Mother!"

"Where did you get that idea, Ingrid?"

"It is indicated in the Bible there. The page was open where Mary Magdalene is honoured as Holy Virgin."

"You must have misunderstood! Magdalene was not a virgin, on the contrary!" Jacob became very serious.

"It doesn't speak of physical virginity. It speaks of pure consciousness that was immaculate. Do you understand, Jacob?"

"You have lost me here. Are you speaking of the Immaculate Conception?"

"Yes, I am! She must have been pure! Why would Jesus love her and allow her to anoint his feet? Jacob, I think that

Immaculate Conception is taking place in consciousness, within the heart. The birth of the Christ Child! The birth of the Virgin of the World!"

I had nothing more to say on the subject. Jacob was thinking about what I said. I introduced him to something that has threatened his programming. I chose not to continue on the subject. I appreciated him as he was. I told him that I had met some interesting people and the guide of "Esoteric Antwerp". He was pleased that I managed to visit Ruben's House.

Our lovely lunch was sealed in our stomachs by the most delicious Belgian chocolates. The master chocolate maker lived in Antwerp!

In the afternoon, Jacob took me to the Institute by Brecht where he worked. The park on the property was absolutely beautiful. Mature trees of many kinds, blooming rhododendrons, and pathways filled with yellow sand. The architecture of the Institute was quite modern. Everything was well planned, with classrooms, gym, pool, dining rooms, and plenty of light coming through many windows.

Jacob showed me the interior of the joined church. It was spacious and magnificent looking. There was an emblem above the altar. I had difficulty seeing at the distance, but have noticed a bird in its center. I asked Jacob what it was.

"It is a symbol of Christ feeding his young by the sacrificial blood of his heart. This symbol can be found in some places that were founded by altruistic families in Europe."

"This is the bird that came to me, Jacob! Is he a heron?"

"No, Sister. He is a pelican, the fisher bird."

I had to sit down for a while. Dizziness came over me. The understanding of my experience was coming to me. I was kissed by a pelican! Who is my Priest? Did I have to come to Antwerp to understand the symbol? Yet, this was just a part of the image the bird created! Jacob sat down next to me and offered to be my confessor.

"Jacob, there is nothing to confess. There is something to share. This bird guided me to Europe and to Antwerp."

"Then you are in the right place. I should show you another building with this emblem. It is on the mansion of the counts of Boeckenberg."

"Where is their mansion, Jacob?"

"In Boeckenberg Park. I am surprised I didn't show it to you. I wanted to."

"You thought of beer! That is why you want to go there again," I teased him.

"It would be a pleasant addition to it. Sister, I know you like symbols. I will show you a small sculpture of Saint Michael in the church of Brecht."

Before we left, Jacob invited me to his residence for a cup of tea. He had to check his phone messages. To my pleasant surprise, he had three flags on his bureau: Belgian, Canadian and Chilean. The rotating globe next to them was positioned on both Americas. Then Jacob opened a pretty box where he kept all my letters. He had them numbered. It was sweet! Doubtlessly, we were friends crossing each other's path.

Saint Michael's statue was just over one foot tall. Michael had his arm positioned as if he held a spear. The sculptor never gave him one.

"What do you think, Sister? Any idea?"

"It reminds me of the wood carving by Rudolf Steiner in Goetheannum. He called it a "Representative of Man". A weary looking man with condemned beings in hell beneath his feet and next to him an angelic winged being. The "Representative" stands in the middle, holding his raised left arm in the same position, having no weapon. I would call him a "Spiritual Warrior". Weapon is the mind and the heart, to love the Truth so much that we'd defend it in the action of speaking, writing, and thinking."

"You make a very good student, Sister. Actually, you are a teacher."

Then Jacob showed me an icon painting where baby Jesus looks very frightened and drops his little shoe. Jacob had an explanation: "Jesus had a vision of his crucifixion that had scared him. He trembled so much that he lost his little shoe."

I really liked this idea.

In the evening, back in Antwerp, I phoned Josef's house. There was no answer. Neither was there in the morning. I felt a bit restless and decided to leave for my trip to Lourdes.

Jacob took me to the train station to make sure that I would leave on the right train to Paris. I had to transfer for Paris train in Brussels. I left some of my luggage with Jacob's parents and brought what I needed for Czechoslovakia. I was going to come back to Belgium before my final departure from Amsterdam. I wanted to spend a few more days in Antwerp and around Jacob's family. I loved their company.

FROM LOUVRE TO LOURDES

FROM the Northern Train Station in Paris I took a taxi to my friends' place. They had a bed for me. After two nights and one day in Paris I was going to take a train to Lourdes.

My friend gave me a ticket to the Louvre and drove me there next morning.

Entering through a pyramid into the museum is like passing through a dimension of time into timeless space where present, past and future coexist at any given moment. I had seen so many treasures of art in my life, always eager to place more of them into my mind's memory. I spent the entire day in the museum, enjoying the exposition and the rooms themselves. Incredible scenes were painted onto walls and ceilings, just to complement the beauty of it all.

After many hours in the museum, I walked through the streets of central Paris. This city is very well planned and at any season is beautiful. Before coming to Canada, I spent two months in Paris. The city was familiar and dear to me.

At the end of the day, I went to purchase a train ticket for Lourdes. I could only afford a one way ticket. It was costly and I didn't have enough money for a return. I decided to trust the Universe and take chances. I had to be in Lourdes!

It was an eight-hour ride. The sky was cloudy; it was about to rain. I just made it inside the cathedral of Lourdes when it began to pour. They were about to commence with the mass. This one was in French. I observed the interior, ceilings and altar. Everything was the way I saw in my Mother's Day experience of 1980! My beloved Priest was behind the altar at that time. Will I find him here again?

I took a seat in one of the pews and gave thanks for being there. The church was filling up quickly. Everyone wanted to be sheltered.

Listening to the liturgy of the mass, I perceived a nice energy right behind me. The male voice behind me sang in a clear pitch baritone and had no problems with French. When we were lining up for the Communion, he waited for me, reserving a space right in front of him. Was he ever charming! About forty-seven, tanned complexion, quite tall. I couldn't place him into any ethnic group. Toward the end of the mass we wished each other peace. I wished him in English, so did he. When the mass was over, I turned toward him with the most common ice breaker,

"You look very familiar to me. Have we met before?"

"I am not sure. Are you here with a group?"

"No, I am by myself." I expected our conversation to continue. Instead, he looked at the black and white tile floor and proceeded slowly toward the door. It surprised me, but I gathered he was in some kind of commitment and chose not to talk to any woman. After I inspected the church, I went outside toward the grotto and *piscines*. The rain subsided. I covered my hair with a long white scarf and wrapped it around my neck. My body was protected by llama poncho I had bought in Chile. The grotto area was surrounded by praying faithful and sick. People were filling up bottles with holy water, or drinking it directly. I tried some too. It was cold, but created a heat in my stomach. I went to buy spring water in the store to use the emptied bottle for a refill of holy water. With my last few franks I bought a baguette that would have to last me up to Czechoslovakia. I had only a few coins left. I could afford going to a public bathroom only twice. Eating sparingly helped. Wandering around the grounds of Lourdes cathedral, I paid attention to announcements presented in many languages. The sound system speakers were positioned in every direction. They announced the Rosary procession by the grotto for the evening. Thousands began to gather shortly after. I was getting cold, so I went to warm up by the candles lit up by worshippers. There were hundreds of them. The place was by the *piscines* and provided a shelter.

Someone sitting on a bench near the grotto shifted to give me a seat. I took my Rosary and participated in prayers and singing. I could see everyone in the procession, passing by me. The Irish chanteuse had a gorgeous voice. She sang a large repertoire of Ave Marias. People were asked to say prayers in their language into a microphone. A male voice prayed Hail Mary in Czech. And more Ave Marias followed. For a while I closed my eyes, trying to feel the crowd and bask in the moment. When I opened my eyes, I saw that nice man in the procession, holding a Rosary and very devotionally praying. I observed his every move, his strong hands gliding on the stone in the grotto, his slow graceful gait, his well formed body. He was rare! Not many of his kind survived the modern times. Then he disappeared in the crowd. There was no way I could locate him again. It was dark and, people covered the grounds everywhere. He was a mystery person, who reminded me of my unusual reaction during the Santiago encounter and the regret I had to live with ever since.

After my turn in the procession, it was almost over. Not knowing where I'd stay for the night, I checked the grounds. Roofed wheel chairs were scattered everywhere. There was one under a large tree that would provide protection for the night. It began to rain again. I went to warm up from the candles again, but people blocked the access. When I approached the place from the opposite side, I was drawn toward a particular spot at the end of walkway. No one was standing there. I stretched my hands toward the heat and light and saw another pair of hands lighting a candle. I looked up and saw that nice man! He was watching me in disbelief.

"My first wish just came true!" he said. "I wrapped a paper full of wishes around the candle. To see you again was the first one on my list."

"What was the second one?" I asked.

"To follow my heart and never give to structured planning again. All my life I have been following the voice of my heart, and now, my psychologist tells me that at my age of forty-six I must make a goal and plan for it. She thought I was immature. Today was my first day of planning. I bought a train ticket to Holland and made reservation for supper in a restaurant. Then I met you at the mass and wanted to speak with you, but couldn't because of my previous commitment to myself. I didn't enjoy one single bite. I thought of you and how wonderful it would be to share a meal with you, speak with you, have you by my side in the procession, pray with you and hold your hand.... My train is leaving in one hour...."

We both felt a sadness of parting, yet, we had just met by Divine Providence.

"I'll walk you to the station. We have one hour." I proposed and walked over to his side of the candle tray to introduce myself. "My name is Ingrid. I also hoped to see you."

"I am Frank. I spent two weeks in silence here. I had to go through this process. You were the first person I really talked to. I knew I would meet you here. I just knew that someone like you was coming. I was in prayer and meditation a lot. You were on your way."

"I arrived this afternoon and am leaving tomorrow. I had to see this place and wanted to be immersed in holy water."

Frank was very happy about my intention.

"Ingrid, it is like a baptism! I went through it twice!"

"Frank, as a good catholic you should believe in one baptism only."

"I do, Ingrid. I wanted to be cleansed in my spirit. You understand, don't you?"

"Absolutely! Who taught you to pray Rosary so well?"

"My mother did! It is her Rosary. When she was dying, she asked every one of her eight children what they wanted. I asked for her Rosary beads."

I was touched by this story. He was truthful. We walked up the hill toward the train station. We talked about our trip to Lourdes and who we were in real life. I told Frank the truth about myself, but didn't mention that I was looking for my beloved. He might have misunderstood. I told him that I was on my pilgrimage.

Frank was an engineer and worked in many countries and just like every other good Dutchman, he spoke five languages. Presently, he was in the process of a change into a more structured and settled life. He lived with a psychologist who was trying to help him with that. He wasn't sure that her ideas were for him.

"My life was rich in experiences. When I followed my heart, I was happy. Now, I am planning. There is no excitement in it and I realized today that it cannot work for me."

"Life meets us, Frank. We don't meet Life. It can actually be harmful to our personal journey to set a program, schedule tomorrows. Life goes from one point to the other."

Frank was concerned about me staying by myself overnight without any reservations for lodging. He wished he could miss the train, but his friend psychologist was waiting for him on arrivals in Holland. He was divided. His heart wanted him to stay; duty called for commitment.

It still rained, but we didn't feel it. Continuing on our way to the train station, we kept on immersing ourselves in each other's energy, without any physical contact.

"You feel like a dear soul to me, Ingrid. For how many past lives have we known each other?"

The street lights revealed the reflection of tears in his eyes. I was unable to hide mine. We had a minute on the platform. The sound of the train brakes cut into our last words of parting. We had each other's address to keep in touch.

I saw him waving while the train went into motion. I watched until the last wagon disappeared on the horizon. A terrible sadness came over me. He was gone.

I walked back slowly. Some pedestrians crossed the street to the other side to avoid me. I guess they didn't trust my poncho. I probably looked like a gypsy. My blond hair was covered; my face hidden under a hood.

There were some people praying for healing by the grotto. I noticed that most of crutches hanging there were very old. Self-healing is a long process. Frank was trying to heal himself, but was already realizing that going against himself will take him nowhere. I went to check on his candle. The flame died. I lit it up again and I watched over it until all of the paper spiralling around it was burnt. I wanted his wishes to come true.

The security guard found me in the cart and offered the use of a mattress by the *piscines*. They regretted they didn't find me earlier. There was more room in the Inn for pilgrims. I was privileged to have a personal body guard. I fully trusted this one! The area was very quiet for fourteen minutes. Every fifteenth minute was filled with the loud Ave Maria played by the basilica's clock chimes. I hoped to sleep for a few hours I had left of the night. I dreamt about people; lots of people. I spoke in many languages to them and I spoke them very well.

Upon awakening, I warmed up with a drink of holy water and went for the first mass. This one was in Italian. I sat at the far corner of the right wing and slept through most of the service. The janitor let me rest until the second mass.

Anxiously, I waited by the gate to the *piscines* for my baptism. A very kind man asked me to sit on a chair by the door just for a moment, until I was welcomed by a nun wearing nurse's uniform. She took me to ladies' section and had me to wait two minutes, during which I had a chance to read instructions. A curtain opened and I was invited in. There were three other women of all ages and shapes getting dressed. I was offered a cape to cover my nude body. With gentle care the nurses helped me undress. They all had consideration for modesty. I waited for my turn. Another curtain opened and the brilliant sunlight beaming through the glass roof embraced me. Three nuns waited to assist me. One asked what language I spoke and I said that French was fine. She asked if I preferred English. I agreed to English. Then she asked me to make a promise to Mary and step into a pool to kiss her statue. At that point my cape was removed from me and two nuns guided me into a cold water pool made of stone, praying for me. After the kiss, the nuns immersed me in the water and offered their hands to lead me out. I was extremely joyous. This was the baptism I wanted! I kept on thanking them. Wearing my cape again, I entered the change room, where equal attention was provided.

When I stepped outside, I felt renewed. It was not a self suggestion. I felt fantastic! I had no other motivation to stay in Lourdes any longer. I walked in the direction of the highway to hitchhike to Bordeaux and then to Paris. It was a long trip and I needed more than luck to get to Paris on the same day.

The first passing car stopped. The driver said he was going to Peau. I joined him, but five minutes later I realized he had another intention. Fortunately, he let me go. I walked a few meters along the highway when a red sports car squeaked its brakes. He was going to Bordeaux. The Portuguese driver must have been a car racer. I asked angels for protection. Again, I was glad to survive this ride.

It was raining in Bordeaux. I walked over a one hour to the exit highway.

Again, the first car stopped. The driver was from Lourdes and was going to Tours, which was much closer to Paris. He was a good man, in his fifties. I trusted him. He invited me for a lovely supper in Tours, passed me his hotel room and the next morning picked me up for breakfast and took me to the train station, supplying me with a ticket to Paris. I couldn't believe his generosity. He was a part of the Providence, no doubt.

I still had holy water and bread for my trip back home.

Magic flute

I TRAVELLED to Prague by train on the day of democratic election. Václav Havel won, of course. I had a precious time with my friends and relatives, visiting places of my childhood and teens, taking pictures everywhere. In June, theatres had last performances of the season and I had a fortune to purchase tickets for "La Bohème" and an Opera Debut Matinée. On both performances I ran into my professor, so he invited me to talk to students at the Academy and surprise other professors. To my amazement, they never forgot the rebel. We had a great time together.

I visited some castles and churches, tasted good Bohemian beer, and enjoyed my visit. The three weeks passed quickly. The visit is worth another novel.

I spent two days in Prague before my departure for Belgium. My dream came true! I got tickets to the National Theatre. It was through a friend who knew that I was coming and she reserved them for me. I went with my two lady cousins.

Our seats were in the first row, centre, on the first balcony. Incredible! The opera? Magic Flute! My favourite! My cousins and I loved the evening. The opera was in Czech language. The original libretto was not respected by the translator. The meanings were lost.

On the way back to Belgium, I regressed in my memory to the "Magic Flute" performance I saw in Canada in the spring of 1989. One evening, after our rehearsal of Bach Choir, I was dropping off my friend Rick. He was a student of music and was blessed with a clear baritone voice. He invited me to join him for the opera.

"You've been a helpful friend and I know you like Mozart, Ingrid. It would be my honour."

It was an emotional moment for me. In those days Verne was difficult, wouldn't communicate, and I wouldn't have had money for a ticket. Naturally, when I was ready to leave for the opera, Verne made inappropriate remarks on my evening of fun without him.

At that time, the "Magic Flute" was the perfect message I needed to hear. The English subtitles provided information I appreciated.

Tamino fought a dragon and won. While resting after the battle, he was found by the ladies who were companions of the Queen of the Night, whose daughter Pamina left home to find Truth with the Mystic Brotherhood. The queen showed Pamina's picture to Tamino, who fell in love with her instantly. The queen wanted Tamino to rescue her daughter from the influence of the High Priest. Tamino searched for Pamina, meeting Papageno on the way, who dreamt about a woman 'exactly like himself'. Papageno married Papagena. Tamino was given a Magic Flute to guide him on his quest. He found the Brotherhood and was instructed to keep the vow of silence. Pamina was informed about Tamino being in love with her and searching for her. She began her own search for him. When he, because of silence, could not answer her, she mistrusted his love and wanted to take her life away. Instructed by good spirits, she pursued Tamino. They found each other and were initiated into a higher level by the High Priest. First, they had to pass the test of Fire and Water. Their love saved their souls and the High Priest gave them the title of the 'noble couple' within the Temple of Isis.

I wondered if there was any coincidence between the name PAMELA and PAMINA. The power of my love for my beloved was stronger than nature's call for union with him. I had to find out who he was and then I'd have peace. My intuition hasn't changed: my beloved was also looking for me, in his own way. He had a name for me. For a while I called him Yariek. I trusted that our paths would cross again.

On my return to Antwerp, I wanted to call Josef's home again and hoped to have some news from Nico or Jan. There was no way I could go to Ritman's Library this time. I couldn't afford a day in Amsterdam! I planned the trip to Holland for the next year. I've met the Dutch Frank; everyone was directing me to Holland. There must be some answer for me in that country! Everything has its time and its season. I was willing to give it time.

HERMES

JACOB was very happy to see me again. I had so much to tell him. The De Schryver family received the card I sent them from Czechoslovakia. I was pretty sure that Frank received his by now, with the Belgian phone number to contact me. Nobody phoned me yet.

Jacob took me to Boeckenberg again. He was such a good listener. Not once would he be judgemental. He heard about Frank, my friends and relatives from my old country, and about other interesting encounters. We walked on the path or sat down on the bench for a while, then walked again. We must have combed the park at least twice. Each time we crossed the bridge, we both looked at the lion crest with Nec Fallere, Nec Falli. Till we walked across the bridge the second time, I remembered the castle of the Counts of Boeckenberg. I became anxious to see their emblem. We walked much faster to the other side of the park. A large meadow spread before us and there was a three story mansion.

Jacob pointed at the emblem above the entrance.

"You see, Ingrid, this family has the same emblem that you saw in the church!"

For a moment I analyzed the connection between a pelican, myself, and to me these unknown humanitarian families. Why was I standing on that lawn at that time? Should I be walking to the mansion door and ask? Ask what? The pelican I'd seen must have represented more than my beloved! I must have looked perplexed, because Jacob took my arm and tried to lead me away.

"Ingrid, this is the right time to have a beer!"

I laughed. The way Jacob said it was amusing and caring at the same time. I let him be my leader.

Conversations across the table have flavour and depth. Social drinking can be an asset. Jacob took in the first gulp of beer. With foam on his upper lip, that gave him the appearance of a wise man, he finally came up with a question.

"Are you sure you know what you are looking for, Sister?"

"Yes and no. What are you trying to tell me, Jacob?"

"Your beloved might have been used as fish bait."

"Fish bait? Fish bait for what?"

I saw a lovely omniscient spark in Jacob's eyes. He took another gulp in and wiped off the foamy mustache.

"To lead you to completion; to make a pilgrim out of you. To be guided by the memory of pure love so you don't have to settle for less."

"I don't want to settle for less, Jacob!"

"You meet Frank, other men are drawn to you; your ex-boyfriends are still in love with you. Don't you get the message?"

"Message of what, Jacob?" I couldn't grasp Jacob's suggestion. At times I contemplated this subject as well. Why am I meeting all these special people? Are they to be my friends, lovers, husbands, teachers, students? What is happening here?

"You are being tested, Ingrid!"

"Tested on what? Fidelity, loyalty, commitment, or what?" Jacob stirred up a defensive force in me. "Don't you see, Jacob, that I am actively looking for my beloved in all the worlds to find him soon, so I can know where I am with him? He may be looking for me too, you know! Unless I know who he is, I cannot commit to anyone. As long as I don't know, I can have fun, that's all I can have...."

"Why don't you have fun while you are searching?"

"Fun is not satisfying, I long for deep love."

"Ha, I caught you! Your longing is spiritual in nature. You long for God's love. It is not about romance, it is about Divine Romance.

Unless you can drink of that cup, you will thirst! I know about thirst, believe me!"

Jacob finished his beer and ordered another one, while I was looking into the settled foam in my stein. The foam formed the outline of Americas within the ring of my mug. When I was about to show it to Jacob, the shape shifted. I was thinking about Jacob's words. Was he leading me into realization of my own quest of the Holy Grail?

"You look serious, Ingrid! I hope I didn't spoil your enthusiasm...."

He clicked his beer mug against mine. "Hey, join me! I cannot enjoy it by myself. Sharing is important."

I pleased him, having a couple of gulps.

"You said it, Jacob! Sharing is the key. I want to share my quest, my spirituality and love. I already found my love, but must find him again!"

"Why did you leave him on that street, then?"

"For loyalty, duty, perhaps. In a way, I don't know why I did it."

"So you can seek on your own," said Jacob, looking directly into my eyes.

"You are probably right, Jacob. All that has happened to me since the encounter appears to be connected. It is like chain link. In a sense, it is magical!"

"The magic flute!" Jacob gave me a wide smile.

"Have you seen the opera?" I asked him.

"A long time ago. Beautiful music .... A very different fairy tale!"

Jacob took another gulp in, waiting for my input. I welcomed the opportunity.

"All fairy tales convey a deeper meaning. They resonate with children's inner psychology. They introduce archetypes to the psyche. Magic Flute is made for adults. It made Schikaneder rich. He got kicked out of Free Masonic Brotherhood for it. Apparently, he was not to reveal some of their mysteries to the public. I believe Mozart was excommunicated too."

"What do you think about secret societies, Ingrid?"

"I guess at some point in our history they had to be secretive, not to pass their knowledge to the profane, but I wonder whether it is necessary now."

"They likely practised that pearls should not be cast before the swine." Jacob concluded.

"Frankly, Jacob, who has the wisdom to select the elect? There are many wolves in sheep's clothing. If an individual is ready to understand the mystery, it will somehow be revealed to them. A man-made initiation in mystery schools is only symbolic."

"Ingrid, did I ever tell you that I appreciate you?"

"Indirectly. Cheers to our friendship, Jacob!" I raised my stein and toasted to this very special catholic priest. He was my pal.

The evening with Jacob's parents was very pleasant. My French had improved from my visit to France and by my immersion in Czech. Through my experience with languages I learned that each time we use one of them, we simultaneously improve in all of them. It must be like a spiral triggering the points in our memory bank, going broader and deeper. The more languages we learn, the easier it becomes to use them. That evening Jacob left for Brecht.

I chose to return to Den Alchemist book store on the following day. I walked by Josef's house and noticed a car that was not parked there before. Spontaneously, I walked toward the main door and pressed the doorbell. The door was slightly open. My heartbeat accelerated.

I heard Josef's voice calling aloud, "Come in!"

I entered the hallway and respectfully waited. A man in his late forties, dressed in overalls, with pliers in his hand, walked downstairs. He didn't know who I was.

I introduced myself. Josef reached for a handshake. He seemed gentle, kind. Fortunately, I didn't feel embarrassed. I apologized for my previous communication. In some aspects, Josef resembled my beloved.

"Did you receive my letter?" he asked anxiously.

"No, I haven't. If I had, I wouldn't have come. Antwerp holds a special post in my life. I had to come."

"Have you found him?"

"No, I haven't, not yet. But I am getting answers. I am on the right track. Thank-you, Josef, for your participation."

"I wish I could be more helpful. I hope you'll find him soon! You'll come back to Antwerp, won't you?"

"I think so. I want to look in Holland, too."

I turned toward the door to leave. Josef reached for my hand and squeezed it very compassionately saying, "I wish you all the best, Ingrid!"

As I stepped over the threshold, I realized that he was another person I inspired to the quest of the true love, that it was worth the effort to find it.

It began to rain. My coat was impermeable and I always carried an umbrella with me. I walked by Jan's house and later on by Nico's house. It took me about forty minutes to get to Green Square in my high heel shoes. I mastered walking in them since I was fifteen.

On the way to the center, I saw many Jewish children and adults. Antwerp seemed to have a high number of Orthodox Jews. Jacob once explained their modest clothing and appearance to me. Women wore wigs. In their tradition, lust had to be conquered by stripping outer beauty and learning to love the essence of the person only. The women shaved their hair and looked very unattractive.

Den Alchemist was open. I was looking around for some kind of message. I picked a couple of metaphysical cards of artwork and noticed a quarterly publication of a magazine called Den Alchemist. Among many issues there were some from the year 1988. I had money for only one of them. I chose the October issue.

On the way back I stopped by Nico's house. He was pleased to see me again. He poured a question at me,

"Have you visited the Hermetic Library in Amsterdam?"

"I decided to go next year, Nico."

"Why next year? Why not now? You are already here, Ingrid! Phone them, make reservation and spend one more day in Holland!"

"Nico, I already decided to come back the next year."

Nico realized that my mind was already made up about it. He couldn't possibly know the real reason. I had no money left. I could only get to the Schiphol airport for my flight. We parted in a cordial way and I promised to keep in touch.

The rain subsided. I slowed down my pace, trying to feel the energy of the city and its connection to my heart. In two more days I was to leave Europe for Canada. I began to miss my children, whom I had phoned a few times. Monica looked after everything. All was well. The children's fathers fortunately lived in the same city and had regular access to them.

Madame De Schryver saved a lunch for me. She was a true mother; caring and thoughtful. At last, I had privacy in Jacob's room to look into my Den Alchemist magazine. It was published by a group called Parsifal. Among the contributing writers were Jan Snijder and Hermes. Who was this Hermes? Quickly, I turned to page with an article called "Totaal Liefdesgeluck". From my limited German, I understood the meaning "Total Love's Delight". I read the article written in Flemish. I understood every word. I felt every line in my Soul! I knew the writer's feelings. I knew him! Who was he who signed by the name of Hermes? He could not be Trismegistus, the thrice initiated one! He was someone who lived in our times and dared to use the pen name Hermes. Could he be the one I was seeking?

My heart was racing. I rushed downstairs to phone Nico. He didn't know him. He suggested getting in touch with the bookstore owner and asking him.

Jan might know about this Hermes! I phoned Jan. He didn't know him either. He said that no one knows who he is in real life. He also recommended asking the bookstore owner.

I phoned Den Alchemist. The kind lady clerk gave me the name of the owner so I could drop off the letter for him with my request. I did it that same afternoon. I left my Canadian connection in it and De Schryver's phone number, just in case.

MYSTICAL MARRIAGE

JACOB picked me up in the morning to take me to a small town called Lier. It was a special place with particular architecture and a charming convent. We listened to the musical clock on the main square, bought some typical Lier pastries, and then went to feast on more of them in a nearby restaurant. I remembered Marc once telling me that his family lived in Lier for some time.

Jacob chose the restaurant. He said he had something to show me there. After we ordered our goodies, he led me into a small room joined to the dining area. There, on a wall, was a large poster with topless women, each of them carrying an oil lamp. Jacob liked the way the artist introduced one of the mysteries to modern man. When we were enjoying the pastries, he asked me,

"What do you think about the picture, Ingrid?"

"Weary looking virgins with oil in their lamps," I answered impartially.

"They don't look like virgins to me! They look experienced in every walk of life," said Jacob, waiting for my more passionate input.

Finally, I was ready to satisfy his expectation.

"Naturally, Jacob. How could they gather the oil for their lamps, otherwise? Only by immersion in real life it is possible, by living it, not escaping it! We don't find it in convents, or monasteries, or by meditating on top of a mountain. I would like to see all those self-righteous men and women to assume the daily responsibilities of today's most of people's lives. Would they be functional, would they have enough compassion and faith to continue to the next day, or would they rather retreat into their 'peace'?"

Jacob stopped savouring pastries, looking at me with that familiar spark in his eyes, indulging in the fire of my words.

"God really took your heart into His, Ingrid! He needs workers like yourself, He needs that extension of Himself. Your lamp was lit when you met your Groom, your Comforter."

The pastries left no more taste in my mouth. The first bite was delicious, but our conversation had taken me to another plane. I was back on the street of Santiago, seeing my beloved, feeling the outpouring love from his eyes. The ineffable longing for his return into my life brought sorrow into my heart and tears into my eyes. Jacob passed me his soft napkin, so I could wipe them off. My internal clown uplifted the mood by a deliberately staged louder blow of my nose. We laughed for a brief moment.

"Except, Jacob, I walked away from my Marriage. Instead of partaking of the Heavenly Meal, I walked away. Maybe, I didn't have enough oil to last me through the Feast, or, wasn't pure enough to be a Virgin Bride. I don't think I did well. I went for more oil, but when I returned, He was not there anymore. If you know the story of the Lord's Brides, I was the fallen one."

Jacob placed his loving hand over mine, which was playing with my clean napkin and folding it into a small square.

"When you met your Groom, you were placed into another World. It cannot be measured by time. What makes you believe that there was some nuptial experience to follow? Your Marriage took place in your heart. You had your wedding night and conceived a child. You had your Immaculate Conception, Ingrid! Do you understand?"

"Jacob, you are an exceptional catholic priest. Where does your wisdom come from?"

"From you, my Sister! Being with you and around you, changes my perception. You are the catalyst. Thank you!"

There was no need to say more. We had shared with each other what had to be said and heard. When there is balance and harmony, the Truth is always present. Every question has its answer, or otherwise, there is no question.

That day was a sweet day. When we returned to Berchem, Jacob's parents invited us for Belgian waffles with berries and cream. In the late evening I tried to play their piano, which was very much out of tune. Nobody had played it for years. I picked a few tunes and ended with Ombra Mai Fu, sending the sound waves to my Groom, wherever He was. The next day I parted with this special family, their city, country, and our continent. I knew that I'd be back.

At the Schiphol airport I had plenty of time to browse around the duty free shops, observing the crowd of shoppers and travellers. I've seen more tall and slender men here than in Canada. Many of them had the same body type as my beloved. Definitely, I was to be back next year.

My children were glad I was back. Monica did an excellent job with the children, household, and money. She actually saved thirty dollars for me, knowing that I would return broke.

Hanna came within days to see photos from Europe, and spent hours on the phone with me, listening to my adventures. She was astonished about the flow of the events and about people I've met. She was hopeful that I might hear from the mysterious Hermes, but strongly believed that I'd hear from Frank.

Ray was quite detached from my story and I began to feel some negativity from him. It didn't bother me. I still considered him to be a good friend, but the gap between us was growing wider and deeper. He was one of those meditators avoiding real life. He preferred to live in the unreality of his own mind creation. I wondered who was more daring. Him, or me? We both were chasing our vision. My subject in my reality was tangible. His subject was tangible in his reality. In a sense, we were doing the same, except, on different planes. How can we tell what is real or unreal? Where does the dream begin or end? The best was to wait for our harvest and its fruit.

Toward the end of July, I was phoned about auditions for a new season. It was recommended that I try for a solo in Bach's BWV 140 Wachet Auf. I picked up the score and the tape with the cantata. "Wachet Auf" means "Awake". It is a message to maidens, Brides of the Christ, to be ready with oil in their lamps for His coming to the wedding feast. Prior to the part I was to practise, was a Recitativo No.5 with a male voice introducing a Duet No.3. At the end of Recitativo, a kiss on the right cheek is mentioned. The pelican kissed me twice on the right cheek! I read the words in the duet. The base voice is of the Bride-groom, the soprano is of the Bride. She asks her Saviour when He is coming and He keeps on answering that He is coming. She was waiting for Him with the lit up oil lamp. He was opening the bridal chamber for the heavenly feast, inviting her. She says "Come, Jesus" and he answers "I am coming to the Feast." She invites Him, "Come, my Saviour, I am waiting with the lit up oil lamp." The duet is a continuing dialogue of the Noble Couple and the melody reflects the motif. I fell in love with the piece! This cantata was about the Mystical Marriage. Even though I didn't get to sing the solo at the performance, I enjoyed being a chorister and one of many Maidens.

J. S. Bach was fond of mysteries. Most of his works are in German, but I was enriched by singing his Mass B minor, that is written in Latin. Something special happened to me during one rehearsal. In the Resurrection part some absolutely gorgeous music accompanies the words "And He ascended to Heaven to sit at the right hand of the Father". I began to grow bigger and bigger, coming out of my seat and rising. Quickly, I grabbed the seat, checking around if anyone noticed anything. Luckily, I was in the last row and everyone was too busy reading the score. Likely, no one would notice it. It was an out of body experience. I began to realize that B minor scale was in resonance with the Earth's frequency. Therefore, our bodies must be in tune with that frequency.

Coincidently, Frank lived on the Bach Street. I wrote him twice, but had not received any answer from him yet.

Bach's music brought a great joy into my life and led me into meeting Archon.

ARCHON

MY family's survival was challenged. I worked hard on generating business with products I had for sale. I had some shows booked prior to Christmas, but was getting stressed out about the upcoming goods and services tax. Regardless of people's opposition to it, our government chose to test our patience anyway. It was implemented and people stopped buying what they could do without. It destroyed many small businesses and entrepreneurs. Before I returned the product to the company for refund, I tried to sell some for a profit. Our financial situation was critical. I needed help.

In the middle of February '91, another unusual dream came. It was presented as the phone call, this time from my soul mate Gabriel, whom I met many years ago in Quebec City at the time of my first divorce. Gabi was from my old country and tried to make living as an artist, painting. He was very gifted. In this dream Gabi was instructing me to take a massage course. He said that I'd be able to provide for my family.

This was the third message I received about the healing arts. The first one came from another countryman, when I was between my second and third marriage. He was an excellent masseur. He kept on telling me that I would make a very good masseuse and wouldn't have to struggle financially. The second message came directly from a friend of a mutual friend, who, for some strange reason, believed that I had the power to heal him. When I put all this together and my impulsive need to touch people, I decided to inquire about massage courses available. The College was registering for the upcoming massage programme next Monday. I went with my only eighty dollars, hoping that the rest could be paid by post-dated cheque. It wasn't possible, but they offered to reserve my registration for the day, if I come up with the rest of tuition payment. I phoned Eduardo and a couple of friends. They loaned me the money and I was anxiously waiting for my classes to start.

We had a very good teacher and soon I realized that this work was 'my cup of tea'. I loved it and was very good at it. My health was affected by previous stress, but the channelling of the healing energy helped me to recover. I was radiant again and could manage with five hours of sleep.

On one evening, I organized a viewing of a very interesting video at my place. A friend recommended calling Trevor, who was interested in the subject. He came. At the door I recognized him from the auditions. He was tall, strong and very handsome. I mentioned our upcoming concert to the group and sold two tickets. Trevor didn't buy any, but kept on observing me and asked me why I sang Bach and what else I was doing. He also asked me about languages I spoke.

The next day Trevor phoned me and wanted to chat. We had a lot in common, I found. I accepted his invitation to dinner he was to prepare himself. We had a good talk about many areas of life and soon we began to appreciate each other's company. Trevor claimed that he had a gift of automatic writing and was called by the name of Archon. When I asked him who called him that way, he had a vague explanation, but showed me some of his writings. He said that he knew ten years ago that I was coming into his life. As a matter of fact, he showed me a paper he wrote at that time describing me, my physiology, characteristics, talents, skills, languages spoken, and I was to sing Bach's music. He played me a tape where an identical voice to mine was singing. He had other sheet copies stored with his two friends for the last ten years. I checked with one of them. She said it was true. I went to see her. She was an herbalist. She told me that

Trevor could not progress in his development without my help and that I was to show him the way and the opportunity to grow. She also said that Trevor had only male reincarnations. Everything else I was willing to accept as a possibility, but this was totally absurd. There was no way to prove it anyway. He was very masculine, but had no problems with woman's chores; neither would he have had a macho personality. In any case, I found the whole story intriguing enough to keep on seeing Trevor regularly. He hoped for a relationship. I told him about my beloved to whom I was committed. On the next date, Trevor passed me channelled material to read. It said that my beloved was on another plane of consciousness and had no incarnation. I didn't believe it and, as a matter of fact, I was upset that Trevor used his 'gift' to manipulate me. I stopped seeing him. He kept on trying to win me back into his life, having more channelled writings for me. I told him that he was possessed. Then he asked me for help. I went. I used a technique similar to Reiki on him. Trevor felt fantastic after the treatment, but the next day he got very ill. He asked me for help again. When I went to his place and embraced him, a gray cold mass of energy exited through his head, causing his body to shiver for a moment. Trevor stood before me radiant, with blue eyes I'd never seen on him. He was absolutely gorgeous! He believed that I liberated him from some dark entity and that I came to his life to heal him. He quit his automatic writing. Slowly, but surely, we were falling in love with each other. It created a conflict within me, but I had to remind myself of experiencing life fully in the given moment of the being-ness with every breath we take. I practised it in my massages, yet had to learn to practise it in my own life. It was easy to love Trevor. He was a beautiful specimen of manhood and, he adored me. Shortly after, he asked me to marry him. I said I'd think about it. I had to consider consequences. I felt I would betray my beloved, whose name and whereabouts I didn't have. I chose to test the situation. I introduced Trevor to my children. None of them felt comfortable with him. Monica was visiting us at Easter, so she met him. Andrew was afraid of him. Sometimes children fear a new family member for selfish reasons, so I decided to give it time. I continued seeing Trevor, but analyzed the situation.

Monica was graduating from the Bible College and I had to make a trip to Swift Current. Trevor wanted to come along. Monica specified that she didn't want him to come. "I don't feel comfortable around him", she said to me. "I don't know what it is, Mom, but be careful, please...."

Over the years, I learned to respect my children's feedback. They can be very intuitive. I went by myself.

Trevor expected me to arrive directly to his house on my return. He had a home-made chicken stew waiting on the stove. He showed me a writing he said he had to do for me. He said it came from an entity called DORMA. I knew from Trevor that he doesn't hear voices when writing. He perceives messages on the feeling level and allows his hand to do the rest. One part of the message was in a strange language. How could Trevor possibly come up with something like that? The message said that Ingrid would recognize the language, but Trevor would not. My intuition suggested that it was Sanskrit. It was phonetically written.

Sure enough, we had an argument over a little thing, just like the message said. I left Trevor's house, taking the writing with me. He gave it to me. I remembered thoughts I had on my return from Swift Current. Something in my heart kept on saying that my beloved was in incarnation and that I had to choose the direction I was to take. The intense love for my beloved was returning and I knew that I had to break up with Trevor. It was almost happening.

I phoned the university and asked the Sanskrit professor about the words in the message. They were almost identical with the slight exception. The meaning was deep, significant, and personal. It was an instruction to me.

I didn't want to tell Trevor about it. He would go back to his channelling and I felt that it was a cause of his problem. He had an addictive personality. I visited with him, though. He was very negative and was sending me away. His eyes and skin colour had changed. His voice was slightly subdued. I offered help. He said I'd better help myself, that I was totally lost with my Christianity and Christian archetypes. I left, but visited with his lady friend, the herbalist. She was very concerned about him and told me more about his past history. She was not happy about his channelling either. She asked if I loved him enough to exorcise him, if he asked for help. He never asked.

I saw Trevor one more time on one very nurturing lecture. The presenter was a true mystic. She spoke about Gnostic writings in the collection called The Nag Hammadí Library. She quoted some lines. It was powerful. Amongst chapters was one on Archons. Trevor and I looked at each other instantly. That was the last eye to eye contact we had.

I have no idea what Trevor had done with the information, but I called the Hermetic Library in Amsterdam, asking about Archons. They said that there is a chapter on them in The Nag Hammadí book. They gave me the ISBN number of the book and offered to send me information on their library. When I asked who the owner was, the secretary said that Mr. Josef Ritman. The stillness entered my being and I began to burn with curiosity. I gave them my address and anxiously waited for the package.

That same day I went to a book store to place an order for the Gnostic gospels. To my surprise, they had two copies in the store, but nobody had touched them yet. I bought both of them - one for me and one for Trevor.

As soon as I got to my car, I scanned the Table of Contents. On the page 161 there was The Hypostasis of the Archons. When I got home, I began to read. I was astonished. They are called Rulers and have a different origin of creation than most of us earthlings. The chapter goes back to Genesis and explains Archons as androgynous, but in male bodies. Their mission here is over once they "Defile the Virgins of the World." They can never incarnate the Soul.

I never gave the book to Trevor. I just couldn't do it to him. Toward the end of summer he phoned me, asking forgiveness. He claimed that he had no memory of what transpired between us. He asked if we can start all over again. At this point I told him that his writing was in Sanskrit and the message was very meaningful to me. I thanked him for it but assured him that our paths had already crossed and we each must move on and pursue our own journey.

PELICAN

A GRADUATION from the Relaxation Massage course was over. Some of my acquaintances gave me a chance to practise on them; some paid me for my service and booked another appointment. I decided to continue with my training and to save some of my earnings for the next course.

I spent most of the summer days with my children, taking nature walks to the nearby hilly natural park. Nose Hill Park is the home of many birds, rabbits, deer, and coyotes. Andrew enjoyed communicating with a falcon that nested in a tall tree. He and Maria liked to throw pebbles into a small pond nearby and to hide in the tall grass. I enjoyed searching for wild flowers which grow there in abundance. Some areas around the pond were too soggy and there I found a batch of clovers. I thought of the good luck a four-leaved clover brings and, passing my hand over the batch, I found several four-leaved clovers! I picked them, dried them in my books and, with the exception of one, I gave the other ones away to share the good luck with friends.

As soon as the mail was delivered, I picked it up. Letters from Jacob were coming regularly. Christian wrote less frequently, knowing that I had found my way. I never received any mail from Frank, even though I sent him a card and a letter with my address.

On the third anniversary of the encounter with my beloved, came a large white envelope with an emblem of a pelican. It was from the Bibliotheca Philosophica Hermetica, located on Bloemgracht 19, in Amsterdam. I received an introduction package from the library Nico wanted me to visit. Before opening the envelope, I inspected the emblem. The pelican was feeding three young, instead of two. All the birds were nesting in a moon crescent that was on top of a cube with symbols of Alpha and Omega. Above the pelican's head there was Sun beaming seven rays at pelicans. An oval emblem was lined by a snake biting on its own tail – the Oroborus. The emblem reflected my 'dream experience' I had on September 12th, 1988, when the pelican kissed me twice on the right cheek! Bloemgracht means the 'canal of flowers'. In my dream I saw a canal and I smelled flowers from every direction. Was my beloved in this library, or was he Josef Ritman himself? I was thrilled! I had no more patience. Action was my only consolation and solution. I was so close to my goal!

The pelican and the dream was my key, so were a "library" and a name ending with "man". The name Josef came across several times, so did Holland!

I sent to Mr. Ritman a letter that would melt a glacier. In turn, I received an invitation to the library, when I visit Holland. This wasn't good enough. I needed to know what Mr. Ritman looked like. I must have intimidated the curator with my question on Mr. Ritman's height, but when I asked who designed the emblem for the library, I was given a name of one gentleman from Antwerp. The curator was kind enough to give me his phone number.

The Belgian designer residing in Antwerp explained that the symbol was very old and that he was hired to do the artwork. I figured that he must have met all the people working in the library, so I asked about a tall man of certain features I specified. He immediately named a nephew of Mr. Ritman, who was in his forties. Within minutes I had his address and phone numbers of people who could give me more information. I had to plan long distance phone calls with a budget in mind.

For the first time in my adult years, I celebrated my birthday. I was forty five! Marc, Ray and Hanna came. Marc gave me a bouquet of orchids. Ray gave me a digital alarm clock and a set of Tarot cards. Hanna had a marble bust sculpture of Jesus and a cake she called 'the sex in the pan' for me. It was so scrumptiously delicious that it almost sucked my glands out! I asked Ray why he chose gifts he gave me. He felt it was time for me to look into the symbolism of Tarot. He had deliberately chosen a Celtic deck instead of the design by Aleister Crowley that I liked. Since I never planned on getting Tarot cards, it became a special gift.

Our celebration was amicably gratifying. We nibbled on many goodies. Ray happened to eat a lot, which was very unusual for him. He'd been a vegetarian for ages and practised ascetic approach to everything. Then I noticed that he'd been going to the restroom frequently, so I asked him if he was feeling all right. He replied that he felt great and enjoyed what I prepared.

Later on in the evening we happened to direct our conversation to my quest. All my close friends knew about my search and liked to keep up with the latest news, since there was always something happening. Ray shared with us results of one of his meditations on the Ritman Library. He said that Josef was a stocky short man. He did some follow up work in opening up the communication between him and me. Obviously, my beloved was someone else and I was to find out soon.

A few days after my birthday I received registered mail from the Library. Included was a Dutch publication called Bres 103 with a long article about the library, many illustrations from the original manuscripts, and a picture of the emblem with the explanation of its symbolism. Fortunately Marc translated most of it. I was ecstatic! My dream was more than a dream. I was truly blessed by uniting with my Soul! At the age of forty-two I united with my twin soul and my own Soul! If a pelican feeding two young in Christian symbolism represented Christ, what does a pelican feeding three young represent in Hermetic symbolism? Why did I think that He was my beloved?

I had to keep communication lines busy, sending questions, expecting answers. Aaron would not agree with me. He would say that

I pushed too much, not allowing the natural unfolding. Personally, I felt I had nothing to lose if I wrote to Adriaan, Mr. Ritman's nephew. I sent him a short letter stating that I'd be visiting the library next summer and would like to get in touch with him. I included my address and phone number. Now, I had three unanswered letters that I had sent to Frank, Hermes, and Adriaan.

GUIDES

IN October Ray asked me to pick up a Tarot Guide book he had ordered for me. He lived in a high rise apartment building and brought the book to the main door lobby - I was in a hurry. When I saw Ray, a shiver ran down my back. His upright posture was changed into the posture of an old man, with a curved back. His complexion had an unhealthy colour and his eyes had lost their spark. Instantly, the word 'cancer' came to my mind. I asked Ray if he was feeling all right. He answered that he had a cold. I gave him a hug that he needed, and left. I shared my concern with Hanna. We prayed for him and I began to phone him frequently. I had to find a reason for phoning without creating a suspicion. A tarot symbolism was the perfect excuse. One day Ray sent me a letter about his work done on my behalf. When I asked him why he'd done it, he claimed that his guides insisted.

"Who are your guides, Ray?" I felt mistrust.

"They're angels. You know that I work with angels, Ingrid!"

"Angels do not interfere this way, Ray! Who are your guides?" I demanded a much clearer explanation.

"Ingrid, I already told you! They're angels!" Ray was becoming upset about my questions.

"What are their names, then?"

"Hugel, Jungel... and others," Ray answered, having already gained his calm.

"How about Huge Jungle? Listen Ray, I don't like your angels. Just because their names end with EL, it doesn't make them angels yet. Remember, angels do not interfere! I didn't ask you, or them, to get involved in my case!"

"Actually, Ingrid, they would like to work with you."

"Since they're your friends, tell them to stay out of my life and if you consent, tell them to stay out of your life, for your sake!" I was really heated up. My intuition was strong behind my words.

"What are you talking about, Ingrid? I worked with them for years! They are angels!"

"Bullshit! They are those rotten dark entities feeding on the ambitious spiritual seekers, who are anxiously waiting for some apparition from the other side and who are gullible because they lack experience. They are sucking energy out of you! Don't you see it, Ray?"

"I've never heard you speak in this way, Ingrid! What's the matter with you?"

"Look, Ray, don't try to sell me your angels. You created them, you deal with them. But I don't like what they're doing to you. They are stealing your life force!"

"They are helping me!"

"To what? Keeping you busy writing, so you cannot have any rest and decent sleep, making you believe that your work has value? They've done a good number on you, Ray!"

Surprisingly, Ray was not upset about my words. He just asked me if there was anything else about the Tarot symbolism I wanted to know. I had no more questions. I wished him peace and hung up the phone. I became even more concerned about his health now. I felt there had been a trade between him and his guides. He used their energy first, now they came back for it. In a sense, they became an extension of his being, and him, being a source of energy for them.

I had no regrets about what I said to Ray. It was the fruit of my discernment and ability to recognize the nature of things. As an observer, I had clarity. I cared for Ray. I'd known him for the last twelve years. The time had come to detach from him and allow him to learn from his own choices. I phoned less. Sometimes no one answered the phone. Surprisingly, it didn't bother me.

Not much had changed in my family's activities. Monica worked in Swift Current, Joe and Jean went to high school now. I continued driving the children to school and attending my classes on some weekdays. My musical activities hadn't changed either. Singing was my daily remedy and the piano became a pleasant companion. Income was still sparse, so I kept our spending low. We were getting by, just barely surviving. Some things had to change. I changed my expectations and began to plan another trip to Europe for the following summer.

Exactly on Monica's birthday, the phone rang when I was already leaving to take children to school. I picked it up. I heard the familiar beeps of a long distance call. An operator speaking in Spanish asked for me - a person to person call from Spain. Being in a hurry, I had little patience. I asked her who was calling and she told me Mr. "X". I had never heard this name and told her that I don't know this person and that it must be an error. She asked for my name again and insisted that the caller wanted to speak with me. I was already hanging up when I heard a familiar male voice that spoke to me a few times in the past, giving me information about my spiritual direction. I hung up. At that instant I realized what I'd done, lifted the receiver, but the line was gone. I didn't even capture what the voice was saying. I rushed to the car to make it to school on time. Did I ever regret my impatience and spontaneity! This could have been the call I had awaited for over three years! I hoped that he'd call back. Hanna was very disappointed in me. She believed that it was a call from my beloved.

He didn't call back. I was learning from my mistake - a big mistake. Someone connected to me was in Spain. Could that be Hermes? Time would tell.

Hanna phoned me about a dream she had about me. She described the room as a European residence where someone was just moving in or out. There was only a chesterfield. A man who looked very much like Ray, but had much lovelier features and a taller figure, was enchanted by what I was saying to him. She described him in detail, sitting on the sofa, listening to every word I was saying. He and I were extremely happy and radiant.

"Hanna," I interrupted, "did I ever tell you that my beloved looks like a better version of Ray?"

"No, never..., does he, really?"

"Yes, very much so. You saw my beloved!"

"He is very much in love with you, Ingrid. His face was glowing. He was totally taken by you!"

"He might be in Europe after all! I am going next summer. I have to go!"

"I can see that. Things will work out for you, you'll see!" Hanna assured me.

Then we talked about Ray. I hadn't been able to reach him for a week now, so I began on phoning several times a day. A few days later I went to his apartment building and asked the manager about him. He said that Ray had been taken to the hospital a few days ago. The first hospital I phoned had admitted him. When I told them that I was Ray's close friend, they had his doctor to phone me back. I was the only person asking about Ray. They thought he had no relatives. The doctor already operated on Ray's prostate. It was cancer and it had metastasized. He said that Ray's heart was very weak.

I went to see Ray that same afternoon. He looked terribly pale, tubes in his nose, an IV piercing his thin arm. I pretended he looked fine to me.

"How did you find out?" he asked.

"The building manager told me. What's happening?"

"They want to give me a blood transfusion," Ray answered.

"Why is that?"

"I am weak. But I have to go through this. Angels told me that I'll go through transformation. This is the beginning."

"Like Lazarus?" Ray didn't respond to this question. "Well," I continued, "Christmas starts next week, Easter is around the corner. Many things can happen. What do you think?"

"I think angels are testing me," Ray said softly.

There was no emotion attached to his words. All of a sudden I realized that he never showed any. He was fully capable of using correct words to say something nice, but it lacked depth. I was looking at a dying man, who denied his heart and sexuality, the exact areas of illness. He lived in his head where all mental processes took place, where he created a scenario of his drama. He decapitated himself from his own body. In order to heal himself, he had to connect to his body, flood it with feelings of love and acceptance.

"Can I come to visit you again? What can I do for you?" I asked.

"You have your own family, Ingrid. Do not worry about me. Angels are looking after me."

"Ray, send them to hell - exactly where they belong. You don't need them. You need to find yourself. Christmas is coming, Advent is here!"

"I'll prove my resurrection. You'll see!"

"That's the ego stuff, Ray. You need to prove nothing. Just connect to the innocence of the child in you, find it in the manger of humility among the creatures of the Earth!"

Ray kept silent. We parted. His doctor was on duty. He was in his late thirties and was generous with information. They wrote my name and phone number on Ray's file, so I could be notified about any change.

Our home was already decorated for Christmas and I had my baking done. The children were about to have holidays and Monica was to come home. A care parcel from my mother was delivered, with some gifts and a large box of chocolate figurines we traditionally hang on our Christmas tree. Among the gifts were two towels with initials in the pattern. They were an "A", and a "D". My Mom explained in the letter that she tried several stores to get initials of my entire family, but after finding many with "A's" they had only one with a "D". She bought it anyway.

I visited Ray in the hospital and brought him some of our goodies and a Christmas card. It was my opportunity to uplift him. I succeeded. The words I'd written were directed to his heart. Ray was in a good mood. He looked rosier after receiving someone else's blood. I came back on Boxing Day. He hoped to be released from the hospital soon.

I kept on coming to see him almost daily before New Year's Eve. The doctor wanted him to try chemotherapy, but Ray was not interested. Ray asked for my opinion. I told him he should do what he felt is right for him. The next day he was released. I made sure he had food in his home and that he was safe being by himself. He enjoyed the attention. We talked about life. Ray had regrets. He said that without family old age is sad. I wondered if he would say anything like it while being healthy. I doubted. I remained a good friend and did my best to assist him. Between my family, work, and music, I could come to his place only three times a week and help as much as I could. He was not getting better, but at least stopped talking about his angels and I believed that he had quit with them.

Ray looked for healing from another level. He wouldn't take Essiac herbal extract, which was known to 'flush' cancer out of the system, but he called a Chinese psychic, who had some interesting suggestions and, after dowsing Ray's apartment, he said that it was full of dark energy. A shopping list suggested two Chinese 'good luck' signs, chimes by the door and windows, and vertical blinds. Some changes had to be done in the apartment and Ray had to give away his beautiful ivy plants and a huge fig tree. They were apparently taking energy away from him. They all did well in my home. Ray loved his plants and sometimes asked me how they were doing. I gave him a regular report.

My classes resumed and I had to take on another part-time job to make the ends meet. I became a waitress two days a week. I had hardly any time to see Ray. He agreed to a home care provider and 'meals on wheels'.

One day a friend came over to my place and complimented the botany of my home, but rebuked me for not watering the ivy in the massage room.

"What are you talking about? I water regularly. Don't you see?"

She touched the soil. It was moist, but the ivy was completely dry, as if life left it. Every leaf was dark green, but dried. An instant thought of Ray entered my mind. Is he all right?

I dialled his number right away. No answer. I dialled many more times that day without results. I phoned the hospital. He was admitted again. He actually called an ambulance the previous night. He had problems with breathing and was afraid that he would die.

This ivy was his favourite and decorated a wall in his apartment ever since I'd known him. He used to tell me that plants are connected to humans on the etheric plane and have a spirit to heal them. At that time he told me about homeopathic remedies and herbalism. The ivy had been fully alive on the previous day! This incident must have been related to Ray's crisis. I told him about it during my visit in the hospital. It cheered him up only for a while. A few days later he consented to chemotherapy.

GNOSIS

A FRIEND who was aware of my philosophical nature had mentioned a Salvadorian group that offered teachings on Gnosticism for free. He said that Juan was a good teacher. The friend offered to put me in touch with him.

Juan happened to live near my residential district, so we agreed to meet in the beautiful outdoors of Nose Hill Park, where our children could have some healthy fun together while we'd talk. Juan had that lively spark in his eyes. He didn't know about symbolism of the pelican, but told me about a library in Amsterdam that uses the symbol. Then I told him that I was planning on going there in the summer. This happened around Easter.

"Well," said Juan, "in that case you'd better view a video I have about this library. It is called "Knowledge of the Heart". It is on Gnosis. Then you can decide whether or not you want to come to our lectures."

"Juan, why is the book of my quest unfolding so easily, page by page?"

"Because you've written it yourself. You already know it. You are just rerunning it in your memory. Do not forget that your body lives in the dimension of time, but your mind lives in timelessness. Your body releases information in time, step by step, page by page. There is a sequence to every event outside and inside you. There are no shortcuts, remember that. You are the actress of your own drama and you are the playwright. The important people you meet are the co-authors of your comedy, if you wish to see it that way."

Our conversation expanded into the areas of our common interest. I anxiously awaited the next morning when Juan was to drop off the video. In the late evening, when I had some privacy, I began to watch. It started with the history of the Nag Hammadí Library and continued into present day Gnosticism and its varied practices.

The third part was on the Hermetic Library. Mr. Ritman was a shorter, stocky man, just as Ray described him. The library's curator was an archetypal man. I could clearly see that I was to visit a true treasure of philosophical literature. The library was financed by Mr. Ritman's company called Ster, which means Star. A tremendous vision and purpose must have guided this man, who accomplished so much. Positively, I was to be privileged by visiting it and reading another page of my comedy.

A'DAM

MY part-time job paid for my charter flight to Europe. I qualified for a credit card due to my employment; a neighbour bought my car. I could afford to travel! I enrolled Maria and Andrew in a summer camp, Jean and the children's fathers would take care of other times of my absence.

Ray's doctor assured me that Ray was going to be around for several months yet, and wished me a good trip. Hanna reminded me to keep a journal and to tell her about every detail on my return. Jacob was excited about seeing me again. I had decided to phone Jan and Nico from Europe.

Prior to leaving, I went to a naturopath for advice on preventive remedies I should take with me on the trip. When she found out that I was a massage therapist, she tried to recruit me to work in her clinic. I told her that I'd consider this after my trip. She was a lovely Jewish lady and we both spoke Russian. She promised she'd teach me everything she knew if I'd come to work with her.

The neighbour, who bought my car, drove me to the airport. I sat down in the waiting area a couple seats away from the nearest person. His ears were plugged with earphones, listening to his CD player. In a short moment he took off the earphones and apologized for loud music.

"Actually, I didn't hear anything," I told him. "What are you listening to?" I asked, knowing that he wanted to start a conversation.

"It is my favourite music - Handel."

"You must like Baroque music, then!"

"All of it, but Handel's is special."

"I know what you mean. Everyone loves his Messiah. What were you listening to, tell me!"

"Guess!" he challenged me.

"Israel in Egypt? Water Music?"

"Close... guess again. He had a mischievous smile. He was about my age, quite good looking. He seemed familiar to me.

"Royal Fireworks?"

"You're getting closer! Guess again!" He was sitting next to me by now, looking straight into my eyes, almost suggesting the name of Handel's composition.

"I give up. I don't know. Help me!"

"Water, Fire... try!"

I felt intimidated. I must had shown a surrender in my eyes.

"Alchemist!" he exclaimed.

"I had no idea that anyone composed The Alchemist! Suddenly, I remembered the Flemish term for a bookstore in Antwerp. "There is a Boek-Handel Den Alchemist in Antwerpen, did you know that?"

"My favourite one is in Amsterdam, called Arcanum," he answered immediately.

"My name is Ingrid," I shook his hand in introduction.

"I am Bertus. Nice to meet you."

I just recalled where we've met earlier.

"You know Marc and his wife! We were introduced once, remember? It was in Banff!"

Bert remembered, but we didn't recognize each other at first. He was going to visit his children in Holland and decide about his family's future. I told him I was going to the Hermetic Library.

We had to get ready for the security check. We saw each other briefly once during the flight. We each had our own destination. He happened to point mine out to me.

Walking with luggage in a European city is not much fun. It didn't really matter where I would be staying the first night, as long as they accepted the VISA card. I found a lovely hotel on the main street near the Centraal Station. I was within walking distance to the library and near the Royal Palace. A little city map, that folded into the shape of a tulip, was a picture worth more than a thousand words.

Eager to take a shower and to slip into something comfortable before the rehearsal of my first visit to the place to which the pelican had guided me, I opened the right panel of the curtain to let some daylight in and see who the neighbours across the street were. I saw before my eyes a sign with the large capital letters KING. When I opened the left curtain panel, I read BURGER. It was the Burger King in Amsterdam. I shut the left panel. I could not afford a Whopper anyway - the price was triple the Canadian one. When I was ready to leave, passing over the threshold of the door, I looked back at the KING that would faithfully await my return.

In the center of A'dam (the Dutch short version for Amsterdam) there was lots of activity. Pedestrians, traffic, tramways, bicycles, red lights, green lights, and hardly any yellow. The words of my mother from my early childhood echoed in my memory once again. Each time I was leaving our house, she reminded me to look left and right before I set foot off the sidewalk. Watch for those cars, she always said. We lived at a busy intersection and had witnessed some ugly accidents over the years.

Ten minutes later, I was coming nearer Westerkirk by Prinsengracht. I had to cross one more bridge, turn the corner, and there was Bloemstraat, parallel to Bloemgracht. This was a district called Jordaan. I walked by the Ster company that had window shutters in the shape of tulips. This company financed the Library's activities. Now I was coming to Bloemgracht. The sound of the street noises, the humid air, the feeling of cobble stones under my soles, and, myself, standing there and looking at the houses across the canal – exactly the way it was in my lucid dream on the 12th of September, 1988! Where was my pelican? I looked around, toward my right, up to the sky. No bird was flying; no man was walking toward me. I was standing there alone, perhaps being observed by someone behind a crocheted curtain through the immaculately washed windows. The houses on the other side of the canal looked just like in my vision, but one of them, with the number 19, had the coloured emblem used by the Ritman Library with the pelican right above the door with written words IN DE PELIKAAN. Tomorrow I'd enter through that door, into the pelican's heart. A great joy poured over me. I was truly living my comedy!

Anxious to turn to the next page, I was inspecting my immediate environment. A pub, an antique shop, and a bridge. This bridge had the name Twelve Lilies! Maybe the next one would be Orchids, or Roses. Well, the canal is called Flowers.

I must have been dreaming too much. An impatient driver honked at me right behind my heels. I quickly jumped to the side, to share the space with trees... and... dog droppings. Just one more scent on the Bloemgracht and a powerful reminder of reality.

Now keeping more to the side, I enjoyed walking through the street of my dreams. I noticed that a couple of houses were offering bed and breakfast. I inquired. There was no privacy in the first one. It was far too modest for the price. No, this could not be in my play. I asked in the other one. This one was in my script. It offered an actual apartment with all conveniences. The price was right! I prepaid one night and reserved for a week. Now I knew where I'd be sleeping, where I'd be going, but I had no idea what was ahead of me. My three-dimensional body needed rest and to become one with the regenerated mind toward the morning.

I could hardly wait to get my act together to please the director and the audience. I had no stage fright; I kept calm, trusting myself. I couldn't possibly forget or skip any of my lines. The stage and I were ready to continue with my comedy.

THE DIVINE COMEDY BY DANTE

My sleep was interrupted by numerous chimes of the Royal Palace's clock. When my North American timed body had finally fallen asleep, shortly after was awakened by the street noises. I got up and opened the right drape panel to see the KING, got dressed, gathered my belongings, locked the door, paid my bill, and on foot proceeded in the direction of Jordaan.

I liked my new accommodation. The bedroom with two single beds attached to each other had an ensuite bathroom and next to the bedroom was a small kitchen where I could prepare my meals. A phone was available by the bedside. On the canal view side there was a spacious fully furnished living room with television. I could see from the window the house No. 19!

I phoned the library to confirm my reservation. They reminded me to come to Bloemstraat No. 15, which was the actual location of the library, though their mailing address was Bloemgracht 19.

I was getting ready for my 'date'. The apartment landlord knew Ritman's family well and emphasized that this library was the only one of its kind, and that people from around the world came to visit and study there. He also told me that Mr. Ritman had seven children and by now had several grandchildren. He held a great admiration for the man and for his family. He wished me a memorable visit.

I rang the doorbell of the Library and announced myself through the intercom. The door buzzed open and I entered. Another door made of glass with the carved emblem of Pelican opened. A receptionist welcomed me, showed me the study area, and offered a brief tour through the library, introducing me to its various sections. I looked around to find some familiar faces. None reminded me of anyone I had met before. I was the only guest at that time. The place was very cleverly designed by the Belgian Eric van den Bossche, who provided me with information earlier. The octagonal white table under a pyramid shaped skylight was the common study area. I was asked to sign in the guest book. I flipped through its pages, looking for familiar names. None rang a bell. I found only one address from Canada. It belonged to Arpad Joe, the well-known Hungarian conductor. Most of the visitors were Europeans.

I picked a couple of books written by a Bohemian mystic Comenius, who lived in exile in Holland and whom Dutch people treated with reverence. The books were in Czech. The Labyrinth of the World is a famous philosophical text.

Since my adolescent years, I felt fascination for Jan Amos Komenský's work. He truly understood the learning process and its integration into our memory, how to learn other languages with guidance of this process, using images and their relationships. I would call it super learning.

The Westerkirk's clock stroke twelve times. The library was closing for a lunch hour. I went to my apartment and had a light lunch that the landlord provided. When I returned to the library, the receptionist brought books to my table that she selected for me. One of them was a treasure. It was full of symbolism used in alchemy and Cabbalah. The other large book had actual pictures of mysteries and archetypes, with explanations in a fine print underneath. I certainly needed several days to go through this material! Page by page, I immersed myself in the symbolism, revealing the sacred psychology woven into our spiritual blueprint, taking us into the Microcosm of the Universe within ourselves. I felt gratitude! How many learned individuals and talented artists compiled these works, nurturing the souls of the seekers of Truth, helping them to remember and to be able to transform their truth! Tears of Joy filled my eyes because... I began to remember. At times, my emotions were too intense and I had to switch to another book for a while. There were so many to choose from!

The library's atmosphere felt sacred; its energy was vibrant. How many other libraries offer an environment like this one? I looked around again and my eyes fixed themselves on two large busts of Lorenzo and Cosimo de Medici, the renowned Florentine nobles who initiated a collection of philosophical writings and sponsored some translations into other languages. Mr. Ritman was doing the same noble work! Florence! I almost forgot! Dante's Divine Comedy! I rushed toward the section with Dante's work. I had several publications to choose from. I pulled out one with drawings by William Blake and another with a picture of Dante on its jacket, the same I'd seen in Duomo of Florence. I took them to my sanctuary at the octagonal table. For some unusual reason, I began to tremble and perspire. I looked again at Dante's face, which impressed both Verne and me during our honeymoon in Europe. Why are his features so attractive?

I read contents: The Inferno, The Purgatorio, The Paradiso. I skipped reading the first two parts, but looked at all their drawings. Hell and Purgatory were of no attraction to me. The Paradise interested me! I read page by page, every line of every Canto. There was enough material for several days. At some moments I stopped reading and switched to the Book of Symbols. Turning pages I found a beautiful snow white pelican sitting on the tip of a steep rocky mountain top, with a walled city in the background in the valley. Below the image I read the words:

"Under the symbolism of alchemical marriage, medieval philosopher concealed the secret system of spiritual culture whereby they hoped to coordinate the disjecta membra of both the human and social organisms. Society, they maintained, was a threefold structure and had its analogy in the triune constitution of man, for as man consists of spirit, mind and body, so society is made up of the church, the state and the populace. The bigotry of the church, the tyranny of the state and the fury of the mob are the three murderous agencies of society which seek to destroy. The first six days of the Chemical Marriage set forth the processes of philosophical 'creation' through which every organism must pass. The three kings are the threefold spirit of man and consort the corresponding vehicles of their expression in the lower world. The executioner is the mind, the higher part of which - symbolized by the head - is necessary for the achievement of the philosophical labor. Thus the parts of man – symbolized by the alchemists as planets and elements - when blended together according to a certain Divine formula result in the creation of two philosophic 'babes' which, fed upon the blood of the alchemical bird, become rulers of the world. From an ethical standpoint, the young King and Queen resurrected at the summit of the tower and ensouled by Divine Life represent the forces of Intelligence and Love which must ultimately guide society. Intelligence and Love are the two great ethical luminaries of the world and correspond to enlightened spirit and regenerated body. The bride-groom is reality and the bride the regenerated being who attains perfection by becoming one with reality through a cosmic marriage wherein the mortal part attains immortality by being united with its own immortal Source. In the Hermetic Marriage divine and human consciousness are united in holy wedlock and he in whom this sacred ceremony takes place is designated as 'Knight of the Golden Stone'; he thereby becomes a divine philosophic diamond composed of the quintessence of his own sevenfold constitution.

Such is the true interpretation of the mystical process of becoming 'a bride of the Lamb'. The Lamb of God is signified by the Golden Fleece that Jason was forced to win before he could assume his kingship. The flying Lion is illumined will, an absolute prerequisite to the achievement of the Great Work. The walled city represents the sanctuary of wisdom wherein dwell the real rulers of the world - the initiated philosophers."

I sat back and tried to assimilate what I'd just read. Every word had a significance addressed to a group of certain attributes and, I was a member of that family. I couldn't read anymore. Intense emotions accompanied by gratitude took over my mind for a while, and I retreated into the center of my own universe. I paced slowly through the library, reading the titles and authors of book covers, remembering. A powerful contentment embraced me and I felt truly at home.

A doorbell rang again. I looked in the direction of the entrance and recognized a tall archetypal looking man. He was the director. The curator informed him in a soft voice about something when he looked in my direction. He walked toward his desk first and right after came over to welcome me to the library. Then he said,

"I hope you will enjoy yourself and will find what you're looking for."

"I already am enjoying myself and finding what I am looking for," I replied.

This was the right moment to give everyone the small gift I brought them from Canada. The colourful geostones of various shapes and natural designs originated in Canadian Rockies were received with appreciation. I had a slightly different gift for the director - a bumper sticker saying 'When God Created Man, The Whole World Rested. When God Created Woman, Neither God Nor Man Rested.' He loved it! The simple bumper sticker eased up the tension between us that started one year ago when I phoned asking questions about Mr. Ritman's physiology. Humour is healing.

I went back to the octagonal table, holding The Divine Comedy. After reading several Cantos, I decided to leave the rest for the next day. I had enough spiritual food in me from that day to last me for a lifetime.

Walking back to my apartment, crossing the bridge of Twelve Lilies, while feeling exaltation. I thought how fortunate are the angels feeling this way at all times in eternity of a timeless dimension! How does one cross the bridge into their world?

CANTO XXV

THE octagonal table was surrounded by the section on Alchemy. I reached for one book written by Jacob Boehme, in which I found actual recipes on plant alchemy, involving the principles of homeopathy. Metal alchemy boggled my mind - I passed on that section. I felt that the older looking books offered more profound information. They were all in French - an opportunity to practise. "The Elixir of Long Life" interested me. Here I read "Knowledge and Wisdom have to go in pair. Knowledge without Wisdom is pure Ignorance itself." I thought of my friend Ray again. He read hundreds of philosophical books, highlighted important passages; always quoting someone else's truth. Being an ascetic, without his complementary female and catalyst, he had difficulty incarnating wisdom, which is of feminine nature. And he had no devotion to Divine Mother, which saved many monks on their spiritual quest. Further I read "The renaissance is triple: first the renaissance of our mind, secondly that of our heart and the will, third is the renaissance of the body. Many pious men who seek God had regenerated in the spirit and the will, but very few had known about corporal renaissance." What is the secret behind the regeneration of the body? I was hooked on the subject. Is the aging process natural? Disease could not be in the Creator's plan! Now I had two tasks: to find my beloved and to regenerate my body. What comes first?

My heart desired to find my beloved first. I placed the alchemical texts back into their section and turned to my already chosen Divine Comedy. Paradise! I must find my Adam in Eden! Canto by Canto, my mind scanned pages to find something familiar. Dante's knowledge came through a guidance of a wise Virgil, but Beatrice - Dante's beloved, had guided him in writing the Paradiso. One powerful encounter with his complementary female transformed the poet into a giant!

I began to read Canto XXV of Paradiso. This one is of the Eighth Sphere: The fixed stars. St. James * The Examination of Hope * St. John the Apostle.

The first six verses drew my emotions into the following: "With a changed voice and with my fleece full grown, I shall return to my baptismal font, a poet, and there assume the laurel crown; for there I entered the faith that lets us grow into God's recognition, and for that faith Peter, as I have said, circled my brow; Thereafter another radiance came forth from the same sphere out of whose joy had come the first flower of Christ's vicarage on earth. And my lady filled with ecstasy and glow ....within the eighth great sphere one glorious great lord greeted the other, praising the diet that regales them there. Those glories having greeted and been greeted, turned and stood before me, still and silent, so bright, I turned my eyes away defeated. And Beatrice said, smiling her blessedness: 'Illustrious being in whose chronicle is written our celestial court's largesse, let hope, I pray, be sounded at this height, How often you personified that grace when Jesus gave his chosen three more light!' "

The words of Beatrice continue to speak to the poet. From verse 103 I read: "And as a joyous maid will rise and go to join the dance, in honor of the bride and not for any reasons of vain show, so did that radiant splendor, there above, go to the two who danced a joyous reel in fit expression of their burning love, It joined them in the words and melody; and like a bride, immovable and silent, my lady kept her eyes fixed on their glory.'This is he who lies upon the breast of Our Pelican, and this is He elected from off the cross to make the great behest.'" Verse number 136 led me to the last words of the Canto XXV. "Ah, what a surge of feeling swept my mind when I turned away an instant from such splendor to look at Beatrice, only to find I could not see her with my dazzled eyes, though I stood near her and in Paradise!"

I read the Canto again, and again, feeling its words in my heart. My meeting with my beloved in Santiago had the same attributes. It was another encounter of the poet with his Beatrice, both experiencing a union in Paradise! The eighth sphere of the fixed stars in the city of St. James, in the winter month of Crab, in the year eighty eight! My christed beloved was Dante Alighieri himself! Was I Beatrice, his inspiration and Sophia?

I looked at Dante's picture. My God, it was my beloved's face! The initials D and A from the towels my mother sent me! What are his initials now? Are they the same?

The visiting hours were over at the library. It was Friday. I photocopied the poem and went to my apartment. As soon as I got in, I called Adriaan's house. A lady told me that Adriaan was returning from a two month business trip that night. I was asked to call back later. In the meanwhile, I phoned Jacob and Nico to tell them that I'd arrive in Antwerp on the fifteenth of July. I had to reserve a few days in the library and be there on the day of the anniversary - the thirteenth of July.

Two hours later, I called Adriaan. He knew who I was and asked me when I would like to meet him. I naturally said soon, that night, if possible. He said that I must be desperate. I told him that I was. We both laughed. He explained that he came to spend three weeks with his family and that they were departing for holidays in the morning, but was open to me and would call me back after discussing it with his wife.

One hour later, Adriaan invited me to his home. His chauffeur was already on his way to pick me up.

I was calm. Adriaan couldn't possibly be my beloved, but he could be a very important messenger. He knew something I needed to hear. The ride to his residence was pleasant, a true sight-seeing tour of the nicer parts of A'dam. We arrived at the cul de sac and entered

Adriaan's family's spacious garden. He, his wife, and other family members shared a peaceful time together around the garden table.

They greeted me very cordially and immediately demonstrated their hospitality. We toasted with wine and got down to the point: why I was guided to the library by the pelican.

Adriaan was a well-read man in philosophies and esotericism, having direct access to the great collection of writings. When we got to the discussion on the Great Work, his wife left to assist their children in packing for the trip. Adriaan was a matching description of my beloved, yet, in a slightly different version. He was a balanced person, speaking from the heart that was enriched with knowledge.

"Ingrid Heller…" he said and smiled mysteriously to himself."You have an alchemical name. INRI, HELLER, HALLO. You were born into the Great Work. Do it, then!"

"I cannot do it without my beloved, Adriaan. I have to find him!"

"Ingrid, Hermes comes to all of us when we are ready. He came to you because you were ready."

"Hermes? He didn't come to me!" I responded, perplexed.

"Yes, he did! The Pelican came to you! He showed you the way!"

"The Pelican is Hermes? He is not Christ?" I felt great mystery embracing me and clarity coming my way.

"Our Pelican is Hermes. He came to you, Ingrid. The Great Work is your own work. You can do it with anyone of your own level. You can also begin to do it on your own. The choices are yours!"

Great news: more responsibility on my shoulders! Cutting edges, and being without a teacher to whom I could call for counsel, is a hell of a path. Doubtlessly, I was fond of adventures and used to a rebirth every morning, not knowing where the next meal was coming from, but learning about the Great Work through my inner guidance and trust, was as challenging as climbing the Mountain by myself in all kinds of weather conditions. I'd better be dressed for the weather! I had to be ready for the unexpected.

After our chat, I parted with Adriaan's wife who was a special woman of noble conduct. Shortly after, I was driven back to my apartment by Adriaan himself. He understood me and helped me to feel comfortable about my correspondence to Mr. Ritman, who was on vacation with his family at that time.

Before going to bed, I read the other translation of Canto XXV. It was more specific in relation to my encounter with Dante in Santiago. How blessed were we! The Pelican is mentioned there, the month of the Crab, and all that happened to both of us! Was he visited by Hermes as well? The fisher bird, the King Fisher to whom Parsifal passes the Holy Grail! The three young pelicans must represent the trinity which an ensouled being incarnates. What was to happen next? Would some writing in the Library give me guidance? Adriaan said that I can do the Great Work on my own, if I chose. Opus Magnum was in the area of alchemy and transformation. Would it be the regeneration of the body? What would the consequence be? Do I want to live another hundred years or more? This must be in the later part of my script. Right then, I was thrilled about the flow of my comedy and some immortality was not to spoil my excitement.

The weekend arrived and I had to give myself time to rest. I decided to become a tourist, visit Museum and cruise on A'dam's canals for a few hours. Even though it was raining, I enjoyed the day very much.

That Sunday night I read the explanation on the symbol of the pelican again. According to it, I had all the tools to start the Great Work by myself. Actually, it was expected of me.

TOLEDO

On Monday morning everyone was in a very cheerful mood at the library. What two days of rest can do to a hard working person! While I was talking to the director regarding a person I was hoping to find in the library, he said that I was the only visitor who was guided to them by the pelican and he felt that I had a genuine guidance. When I was describing my beloved to him and said 'taller than you', he heard 'Toledo' instead. My accent gave me away many times in my life, so I chuckled and corrected his misunderstanding. At that very moment the curator was standing next to me, holding a newspaper clip and exclaimed, "It is Toledo! Look!" and she showed me the article.

I immediately lit up. "Thank God! You both are messengers!"

They smiled and said that there are no coincidences.

The article was about a Dutch curator who was doing a translation of some old scriptures in Toledo. His last name was Keller - a very similar name to mine. Obviously, Toledo was my next destination. The phone call I received from Spain some twenty months ago still boggled my mind. I felt that Spain had some answers for me, so I decided to travel there on the day after the fourth anniversary.

In the evening I called Nico and Jacob to tell them that I'd visit with them on the way from Spain. My Eurorail ticket could take me anywhere. I just had to pay an extra fee for the couchette.

I phoned the Gnostic group in Madrid, to which I sent a letter from Canada. Juan supplied me with addresses of Spanish and Dutch groups, just in case I wanted to meet them. Alberto was the person assigned to be my guide once I arrived in Madrid. He had a very pleasant voice. The following day I bought a ticket and reserved a bed for the overnight train from Paris to Madrid. Everything was in place. I still had plenty of time to study and prepare for the day of anniversary.

On the day of July 13, 1992, I was full of expectations. Generally, very few people visited the library, since it was private and promoted by the word of mouth. The staff and volunteers kept very busy there with transcriptions and translations. Many visitors would slow down their work.

I immersed myself in reading Corpus Hermeticum, comparing the text with Gnostic teachings and opening my mind to this source of philosophy. Paragraphs on alchemy and healing fascinated me. There was another earnest student at the library who took notes, just like I did. He was a gentleman in his sixties. At the end of the day, when I went to place borrowed books into their designated section, I had to pass by him. He smiled. I could feel a peaceful breeze from him - a very nice energy. He was reading Paracelsus. He left while I was talking to the curator about my trip to Spain. She wished me a wonderful trip hoping that I'd find more answers.

Then I walked toward the door. The older gentleman was waiting there. I thought he was reading something interesting by the entrance. When I picked up my umbrella from the rack, he asked me if he could walk with me to the train station. When I asked him why, he replied that he would like to speak with me.

We stepped out and I covered both of us with my deep pink umbrella, which projected a healthy glow on our faces. He kept on looking into my eyes and smiling.

"What brought you to this library?" he asked.

"Guidance. I just had to come. I had to be here today."

"Why today?"

"It's a long story. I was to meet someone here. A messenger, I guess."

"People come here for all kinds of reasons. I come here to learn about natural healing. I am writing an article on Paracelsus, so I came to do some research."

"Are you a writer?" I asked.

"No, I am a naturopath, but I do some writing for health magazines. What is your line of work?"

"Right now, I am a massage therapist, but I'd like to study naturopathy in the future."

"I think you should. You have nice energy. Could we keep in touch? I'll give you my address in Amsterdam. Will you write me?"

"Yes, I will write you."

He wrote down his name and address and emphasized the meaning of his surname. When I broke his name down, it translated HER MAN THE DUKE.

"Now, can I walk you to the station?" he offered.

"But, I am not going to the station, Herman!"

"I thought you were going to Spain," he answered.

"Were you eavesdropping?" I smiled while telling him.

"While waiting by the door for you, I overheard your conversation."

"I'll see you on my return from Spain, Herman. I should be back on the 21st. It is the day of my departure. Do you want to meet me here around eleven in the morning?"

He was very happy about my proposition and agreed to meet me in the library. Then he gave me a little good-bye kiss, wishing me a magical trip.

The train from Brussels to Paris was delayed upon its arrival. I only had thirty-five minutes to get myself from the Gare du Nord to the Austerlitz station. The Metro connections were poor. I had to take the last section by taxi. I just boarded the train when it began to move. We were arriving in Madrid in the morning. I had a good Toledo connection. The ride was about two hours long, but not as interesting. Toledo was the highlight. The train station in Toledo is ancient, built in a gothic style. The main hall looked like a chapel with the stained glass windows.

A bus took me to the center of the city. I found a hotel that accepted VISA and since the hotel was going through renovation, the price was very reasonable. It was named Carlos V., after the inquisitor king. My room number was 207.

Almost immediately I looked up Dr. Keller's name in the phone book. He lived on a nearby street. I walked over. The windows of his apartment were decorated by planters with red geraniums. The Dutchman had his garden! He wasn't home. A tenant who lived in the complex gave me Dr. Keller's number to Madrid, where he worked on weekdays.

I reached him by phone. I told him that I had heard about his work from the people in the Hermetic Library and he said that he did some work there in the past and named me the people we both had met. I told him that I would like to meet with him and discuss something of mutual interest. He was coming to Toledo for the weekend and promised to pick me up in the hotel.

I also phoned Alberto. He offered to meet me in Madrid's station on Saturday afternoon.

I enjoyed walking through narrow streets of Toledo, browsing through many stores selling artefacts of gifted local goldsmiths. It is a very peaceful place built on a fortress, uniting Spanish, Moorish and Jewish cultures. Toledo has a rich past. Not all of it was good. The Inquisition Council had its headquarters there and many bloody tortures had been performed right there. Interesting, how a doctrine of the Catholic Church hoped to be spread all over the world by force and by creating fear. The best of the crop, including the most advanced minds of that time, such as inventors, thinkers, and Cathars, were all being persecuted and eliminated in the cruellest of ways. Toledo's enormous cathedral still emanated horror and shame. I felt much better on the streets among pedestrians, tourists, and merchants at any time of day and night.

Dr. Keller met me in the lobby, as he had promised. He was tall, very handsome, and friendly. We went for refreshment to the main square patio restaurant and had a good conversation. He couldn't presently recall anyone who resembled the one I was describing, but wanted to keep the lines of communication open. I gave Dr. Keller my Canadian address.

In the afternoon I took train to Madrid. Alberto was waiting. He was charming and I trusted him from the very beginning. I had the intention of going to the El Prado museum, but they would close the door in one hour. Instead, we went to the botanical gardens next to it. Alberto was so different from other men his age. He was twenty-one years younger than me, yet had the maturity of a forty year old. He was an artist; a painter and musician, and he loved J. S. Bach. He understood Bach's spiritual and musical genius. Alberto was aware of Bach's passion for numerology and its application in his compositions. Alberto was specializing in aerographic paintings and had created many impressive designs. He was very dedicated to Gnostic teaching and practised what he learned in his own life. Because of his maturity, he had difficulty relating to women his age. I cherished the time we spent together and regretted when our day was over. In order to stay in Madrid until Sunday, I needed to find a decent and reasonable place. Nothing was available. I chose to go back to Toledo, since my night was reserved there anyway. Alberto decided to join me. His mother was from Toledo and he loved the city as well. We needed more time together, to get to know each other better. We truly enjoyed each other's company and shared many ideas.

Alberto booked the room 306 in the same hotel. He pointed out to me that our room numbers totalled 9. We walked and talked until we got hungry. I loved the gazpacho soup we had! It was so refreshing in summer.

Finally, I asked Alberto the question that waited to be popped out at any moment. He knew someone who matched the description I gave him. He said that his name was Ariel. When I asked him whether or not Ariel travels to Chile, he said that he travels to Argentina to Cordova, where his family was from. Ariel was about forty-four years old.

"Where is Ariel now?"

"In Madrid. You can meet him tomorrow. Our group is going to the mountains. You're invited. Some know that you were coming and they would like to meet you."

"Alberto, I don't have proper footwear for that. Tell me more about Ariel! What is his profession?"

171

"He is a waiter!"

"Why a waiter?"

"His family owns hotels. He is making sure that all goes well. He is also a devoted Gnostic. He actually introduced me to the movement in 1988. He was my instructor and a friend. He still is."

For the first time during my search I found a matching description, a name that could well be Yariek, but the surname didn't match my expectation. I could meet this person the following day and yet, I felt that he was someone else. I stopped asking about Ariel and showed more interest in Alberto and his inner beauty, which reflected on the outside as well. I offered him a massage and he gladly accepted. It was more my treat than his. He was fully relaxed and took in what was available to him. My hands sculpted his young beautiful body into a perfect image of Adonis, to remember forever and behold. He rewarded me generously. He gave me one of his paintings, portraying our solar system within the Milky Way. There was his signature: Alberto Blázquez.

I decided not to go to the mountains. Alberto stayed with me until my train to Barcelona was about to depart. We both liked each other very much. I wished we could've been more compatible in age. At all times I was watchful not to ignite a spark of intimacy. It would have been easy to love him and create a relationship. We shared peace and harmony, mutual interests and philosophical belief. What a dear soul I had to leave behind!

Barcelona was the best city of Spain for visitors during this last week of preparations for the Olympic Games. The policing presence was everywhere; the city was spotless and people were extremely friendly. I have very fond memories of that Catalan city.

The Winter Olympic Games in Calgary in 1988 made my home city a better place and since then its friendliness grew. Each time people of various backgrounds gather in a name of unity, it lifts the mass consciousness to reach a higher level.

FROM ALBERTO TO ALBERTA

I TOOK a night train from Barcelona to Paris and from there another one to Belgium. I had about twenty hours left to spend in Antwerp. Nico was in England and Jan was on vacation at this time. Jacob was available. He was sad that we had very little time left to catch up, but was happy about the progress I was making in my quest. He invited me to Brecht. This time we didn't go for beer; he treated me to coffee and pastries in the local coffee house.

We still had that unique fraternal rapport. That likely will never change. He was skeptical about the Dante and Beatrice incarnations, though he acknowledged how incredibly everything fitted the sequel. Intuitively, Jacob was accepting the reincarnation concept, but his carnal mind fashioned by Catholicism opposed his perception. I let it rest and changed subject. I just told him that the pelican in the Library's emblem represented Hermes. Jacob was not interested in hearing about Hermes. He felt it was connected to practices of magic and, he feared it.

I stayed overnight at his Mom's. His father passed away just a few months ago.

The next morning I was on my way to Amsterdam and to Canada. I fell asleep on the train and mistakenly got off in Rotterdam. The next train to Amsterdam was a slow detour train; I arrived at the Library for the afternoon. I had to leave in less than two hours. The secretary had two messages for me. One was from Herman, who waited for me until noon. He had patients for the afternoon and couldn't come back. The next message was from a person unknown to me, who actually called the Library before my departure for Spain. He wanted to talk to me. I called him.

He spoke very nice English and had a lovely and trustworthy tone of voice. He was from Rotterdam. I told him that I was leaving for Canada and had to be at the Schiphol airport by five at the latest to check in my luggage. He said he would wait for me at quarter to five at the meeting place. When I asked him how I would recognize him, he said not to worry, that he would recognize me. I liked this mystery man! Whoever he was, he was in my script! I didn't feel at all that he would be my beloved. I felt he was a very important messenger.

After making a few more photocopies of writings and sharing a bit of my Spain adventure with the curator, I was on my way to the airport. Curious about my new messenger, I truly wondered how anyone who hadn't seen me yet could recognize me.

I was approaching the popular meeting place full of people. Sure enough, a tall man in his late thirties was walking toward me. He had dark hair and glasses.

"Are you Ms. Heller from Canada?" he addressed me.

"Yes, I am. How do you know about me?"

He showed me a letter I had sent to the Rotterdam Gnostic group a while ago. He was their instructor. Now I was clear about the mystery. His name was Juan too! He figured that I didn't have enough time to visit with their group, so he decided to meet me personally.

"How did you manage to recognize me?" I asked.

"I could identify you in the crowd, Ingrid. I can tell a Gnostic!"

"But I am not a Gnostic," I corrected him.

"You are not? What are you, then? What are you seeking?"

"I cannot label myself. I don't want to label myself. I am seeking Truth - the knowledge of my heart."

"That is Gnosis, Ingrid." Juan answered with calm confidence.

The public announcement reported a four hour delay of my charter flight. I checked in my luggage and accepted Juan's invitation for a beer. A good conversation was destined to follow.

Juan asked me why I visited the Library and how I found out about it. I told him that a few years ago I saw the emblem and later on found out that it belonged to the Library. I also told him about the Gnostic video Juan in Calgary loaned me.

Juan glared at me as if he knew I wasn't telling him the whole story.

"Ingrid, you are looking for someone, are you not?"

"Yes, for someone I had already met four years ago in Santiago de Chile. I truly believed that I would find him in Europe."

"You will find him when you least expect it. It can happen in your own living room."

"If it would be that easy, why am I making this trip, seeking?"

"It is the search of your-self within yourself, Ingrid. You probably look too much for him outside yourself....Is he your beloved twin?"

My eyes must have answered it all.

"Do you truly love him, Ingrid?"

"What a question! Of course! I love him the most of all people on Earth."

"Then release him. Let him go!"

"That is too much to ask of me right now. He is with me, always on my mind!"

"Do you want to find him?"

"Of course, I do! That's why I am here, Juan!"

"Exactly! You have to transform it by letting him go and stop looking for him."

I began to cry. Juan touched my hand and compassionately resumed his message.

"Ingrid, by letting go and releasing him, you step to a higher level. Each time you want to transform something, you also must clear its past, let go of everything. He is waiting on a higher level! He is not on this one anymore! That happened in Santiago. Move upward. Climb the mountain! If you just knew how blessed you are!"

"Juan, how can I possibly release him? How can I do it?"

"Love someone else!"

"I cannot love anyone else. He is my ultimate love!"

"You said it: the ultimate. It is in your future. You can have other relationships before him. Try! It is worth trying. You are loving, attractive; you will be able to create a relationship with someone else. You will see!"

"I've met some lovely men on this trip. One of them is Gnostic and knows about sacred matrimony."

"Perfect! Start right there. The magic will happen."

I observed Juan while he was talking to me. He had that same spark of light in his irises I noticed in the other Juan and in Alberto. All of them worked constructively with their sexual energy. They didn't waste. They used it for their own regeneration.

"Ingrid, what if your twin is married?"

"I doubt it. He had no ring."

"In some cultures men do not wear one. What if he is married?"

I didn't feel very comfortable about it. On the other hand, I was relieved. It actually felt liberating that my twin would have someone to love him, to care for him, and hopefully be the mother of his children. I knew that my beloved lived in denial in the past lives and needed the balance and grounding that married life sometimes provides.

Juan inspected my eyes, noticing that I was thinking about this possibility. "Ingrid, you did not answer me yet! Would you pursue him if he was married?"

"No. I would adapt to that. I would love to be his and his wife's friend, though."

"Good. You are ready then."

We paused for a while. I wondered whether Juan's questions were suggestions, tests or messages. Then I asked him about his path and Gnosticism. We ended up talking about alchemy and alchemical marriage.

Juan had to go back to Rotterdam. He was teaching a class that night. Later on, I received a lovely card from him with words of encouragement and friendship and an instruction "Teach your beloved the path of sacred matrimony".

The charter flight was delayed another three hours. I arrived to Calgary in the early morning. Eduardo was kind to pick me up and to take me to my children, who were waiting for me since last night.

I thought a lot of Juan's words and sincerely tried to follow his instruction. I could not live with an empty heart. As far as I remembered, I always loved someone. If it wouldn't be my cousin, it would be my teacher, then some movie star, my brother's classmates, and near the age sixteen I began to date real people. My heart has always loved someone. In my troubled marriages my love was channelled to my children. Love was the essence of my living! There was no way I could empty my heart in order to transform the present situation. I had to replace my beloved.

On the day of my arrival, I phoned Alberto. He was ecstatic that I called him. He said that he missed me and asked how I felt about the two of us. I told him the truth that I cared about him and felt lots of love for him. He cried in joy and exclaimed couple times "I knew you would love me, I just knew it!"

I wrote Alberto a letter that same night. I had to be realistic. The age difference was scary. Many people on the Path claim that age doesn't matter. It did with me. I had children and I had to set an example. Monica's boyfriend was Alberto's age. My letter didn't come out all so negative. There was a bond we had revived in Spain. It was a profound connection, where identification of any incarnation we might have shared made no difference. Together we had experienced the unity that all people will eventually reach when they learn about unconditional love and reverence for each other, for there is a divine spark in everyone. I felt love for my artistic friend whose spirituality reflected in his work and in his countenance.

ARIEL

A DAY after my arrival, I received a phone call from the lady naturopath. She asked when I'd be able to start at her clinic. I explained my situation to her. I had no car, no money to buy one, and my home was far from her clinic. It would take me more than two hours by bus each way. She was generous and offered that if I worked with her, she'd co-sign a loan for a car. Eduardo loaned me his old car in the meanwhile. He used another one. I was mobile and able to start the job.

I liked the work and soon got used to the international clientele she had. I was becoming very involved with my training and that way I kept my mind off relationships. I was focused on my future profession and on my children. Ray's condition was stable, which contributed to my peace. I was also doing internal cleansing with colon irrigations and followed a diet rich in minerals. I started with regular morning exercise and soon I began to feel more energetic than before. All was going smoothly and well.

Two weeks later, I had a very vivid dream where Alberto ran toward me, joyfully exclaiming in Spanish: "Ingrid, Ingrid, it is Ariel, it is Ariel! He remembers you from Santiago! He remembers you from Santiago!" With it came a very loving energy. Alberto held my right hand when he passed me the second half of the message. I was filled with ardent love again. The flame that was slowly dying in me was rekindled and growing. I wrote Ariel a letter the next morning, sending it to the Gnostic group in Madrid. Maybe it was him and I was not ready to meet him while in Spain. I remembered that Aaron told me once that it made no difference where I look for him, that eventually he'd pop out of my interior and I'd meet him in my own living room. Juan said the same thing.

Was Ariel coming back because I released him? Was Alberto's role to enchant me with his inner and outer beauty so I could make this important step? Would my bodily cleansing change my frequency and help me to get to the next level? Whatever it was, I was filled with life again. Clients noticed my radiance and I credited it to the cleanse. Everybody wanted to do theirs. I was their inspiration!

The week passed. Hanna came back from her vacation. She was overwhelmed with my story and insisted that I must write a book about my journey. I received letters from Jacob, Herman, but none from Alberto. His painting decorated a wall in my massage room, where I slept. He and Salvador Dali became my favourite Spanish painters. I was fond of art. My walls were covered with copies of masterpieces, some special originals and a series of Art Nouveau by Alfonse Mucha. I loved my home full of music, artwork, books and children!

On Friday night I waited until midnight to phone Alberto. I didn't want to wake him up too early. I was a sweet awakening for him. He already received my letter and was to write me back. We talked about us and the possible conflict due to our age difference. Alberto still believed that it should create no problem, but I could feel that he wasn't as certain anymore. Then I asked him about his friend Ariel. He was presently in Argentina. I asked Alberto if he possibly knew where Ariel was in July of '88 and he answered with certainty that he was in Madrid.

"But how can you know, Alberto? It's been four years!"

"Ingrid, exactly at that time I joined the Gnostic Movement and Ariel was my number one teacher. We worked together in the hotel at that time. I know he was in Madrid!"

There was very little left for me to say. I was disappointed with my dream. Dreams used to be such a faithful guidance and now they were misguiding me. I had to release all: Ariel, Alberto and any potential partner. It was a week of death. My heart turned into an empty chamber. There was a void.

The lady naturopath noticed that something was missing. The next Thursday she asked me why I didn't date anyone. I told her that the one I would love to be with I hadn't found yet. She said that she would find me a good Jewish man. She was Jewish; I was not. I told her that my man is someone very special and that I chose to wait for him and no one else, but presently, I had many other things to do in life and a relationship was not a priority.

My friend Val called me on Friday night. She'd been a caring friend since I'd known her. This time she was concerned about my education. She offered money for my pathology class so I could continue with studies and earn my diploma soon. I told her about the dream I had and how it turned out. She knew about my quest and assured me that something special would come out of it. Then she suggested dating someone anyway.

"No, Val. I am not ready for anyone else. Not yet. I'll transfer that love to my friends, patients. It is not going to be that difficult. My work takes me in that direction. I'll be fine, Val. I don't feel lonely. I work with people, have four children at home and am very fortunate to have friends like you."

She wished me good luck for the auditions we had on Saturday. Music filled me again. In the morning I practised several of Bach's pieces at the piano and added my Ombra Mai Fu. This time I sang it to the world. My voice was ready.

At the auditions I sang Suscepit Israel and some randomly selected pieces from other cantatas. I was invited to come back to rehearsals. There were some new lovely voices at the auditions. Our new conductor was an accomplished pianist and had very lovely energy.

Andrew and Maria went with Eduardo for the weekend and I was left with Jean and Joe till Sunday morning. We watched the English comedy The Faulty Towers. Did we ever laugh! I needed humour and laughter. It was healing. It was a marvellous day.

By Sunday noon all the children were gone and I was alone in the house, having plenty of time to myself. For the first time in my life I had no desire to do anything. I was sitting on the sofa in the living room, staring ahead of me, oblivious of my surroundings. The feeling of absolute emptiness was close to the vegetative state of absent mind.

A sudden impulse came, as if someone just turned on my personal light switch. I turned on the radio to fill the room with life. A very sweet energy poured over me at that moment and I rushed to see myself in the mirror to witness the Soul presence within my body. I was glowing! I heard an introduction to the "Writer's Company" and to the guest writer, poet, and the playwright Ariel Dorfman, born in Argentina, a Chilean citizen, who was a visiting professor at the Duke University. I heard my Ariel's voice! It was the voice I heard on inner levels! The interview was dynamic. How can anyone answer the way I would have answered? And his manner of speech was similar to mine! He recited poems from his collection The Last Waltz in Santiago. The poem Vocabulary mentioned our encounter! I finally got the idea to tape his voice. Other books and his successful play Death and the Maiden were named. I wasn't myself. I was half stiff and cold, touched by a magic wand. I wanted to drop to my knees and thank God for his guidance. I wanted to shout in joy, compose my first symphony, write another poem. I wanted to make this day of August 29th of 1992 memorable to the world. Ariel! What a beautiful name his parents had given him!

I phoned Hanna immediately after the program. She was excited and exclaimed, "The best news in years! This is him!"

I played her the tape through the phone receiver. She was even more positive then,

"It is your voice in a masculine version, Ingrid! It is like listening to you! Oh, this is exciting!"

Hanna was truly happy for me. When Jean and Joe returned from their Dad's place in the evening, I asked Jean to borrow Ariel's books from the library for me. On Friday she brought me The Last Waltz in Santiago and reserved The Hard Rain, My House Is on Fire, Mascara, and The Last Song of Manuel Sendero.

I looked at the book's jacket and held before me the image that enchanted me four years earlier. Poems like Habeas Corpus and

Something More than Lightbulbs tore my heart. He has been in turmoil, just as Ray told me. Then I read Occupation Army: "On this street corner in Santiago, Huérfanos - Ahumada distance dries out and piles up. Each time you pass by, like a broken record that someone tries to play just one more time. What we lived there, leaps out to hurt you. Everything you had to forget, day by day. That memory comes back to me too. Slowly, suddenly, I am the echo of a record that breaks and that is only played very, very softly whenever a train goes by. In Santiago you go past that corner. I cannot."

He's been looking for me through his poetry, while I'd been seeking places, asking the guardians at the gates about my consort King! Now I had to find the way to his Kingdom. Does the man of exile have his Kingdom?

My comedy reached its highest point. My dreams and guidance had never failed me! How could I ever doubt? The messengers came my way! I was the author, actor, and director again. My Dante came back! The A and D woven into the towels my mother sent me! ARIEL, the name given to the winged LION of God.

PAMELA

THERE are stories that are sacred and must be kept secret. The profane should never know about them. How could they possibly understand, being so far from the Truth? Some stories are sacred, but must be told. The seekers on the Path to completion need an inspiration.

I was holding The Last Song of Manuel Sendero that claimed to be a best seller. There were chapters on Incarnation and many Outside and Inside stories, and much more. I was anxious and read through the pages. The story of David had to be told. The story of Manuel and his love for his twin Pamela intervened with David's. I reached page 34 and read about the encounter of the two souls who broke the rebellion of the unborn against the incarnation and chose to be born to change the world. Pamela went to experience her life in Chile first. Prior to her incarnation she agreed to meet Manuel in the downtown of Santiago where he located her in the crowd of nearby demonstrators. He tried to tell her that he had known her for a very long time, since they were very small. At first, Pamela didn't believe him, but when she experienced telepathy with him, she understood and believed.

The book was written in 1982, when Ariel was in exile, living in Washington D.C. I was living in Chile, working the land, giving birth to my brave Maria, who came to this world in a lotus position. I came in first and it was my responsibility to meet him. Six years prior to our encounter he wrote about us. Hence comes the name Pamela.

Ariel - the man who knows his script, the director, narrator, and the actor committed to his comedy. From the Exile he returned to Eden to experience Paradise, because he had already eaten of the Fruit of Knowledge of Good and Evil, completing the cycle, according to the Law. Being no more washed by the Waters of Lethe, preserving the memory of the Past, Present and Future. The unfinished had to be completed on a personal level; relationships with all kingdoms of nature and the service on the levels that are reserved for the Kings. The voice of Manuel SENDERO, his song and word, the Logos.

All my dreams, guidance and messages came back to me in a flash. All were genuine and true. Did I really have to wait for four years to find out? What would happen if the story continued the way it is in Ariel's book on the following pages? Would the attraction satisfy the longing of the inner doves? In divine comedies there are no earthly duties. The magic flute would play her tune and the test of fire and water would have to be passed.

Truly, I could not imagine my possible reaction, if we had begun to talk on that street location. I would likely do something unusual, totally original and out of this world. Would that be a line in my comedy? What had taken place in my script was correct. Ariel calls his novel a fiction; I call mine a true story. A fiction writer is frequently ahead of his time. He can be a genius, inventor, or a prophet.

I was compelled to call the Duke University. I called and succeeded in having a good conversation with Ariel's secretary. I left the message and began to prepare a tape with spoken letter. I was ready for the unexpected.

All my friends were an encouraging influence and some could not understand why I didn't travel to Durham. My reply was simple: my comedy was developing so nicely, I was not going to rush it and have it over with. There is time and space for everything and my microcosm was to reveal the right time to me. I had professional plans; I had to become financially independent and much wiser.

There was no rush. Besides, Ariel had two sons and a wife who had stood by him through the harrowing times of the exile years. She was his woman. I was not. She gave him children and freed me of that responsibility.

I mailed the tape to his office and had all the time in the world for his answer. The ultimate, the best is for the last. My task was to fill in the lines between the unspoken, verbalize them clearly and live them fully.

I thought I had everything under control. I found my man. What then? Was I supposed to wait for him for the rest of my life? Could I have other relationships before him? What was going on in Ariel's mind? Was he going to write, visit, phone? Was I to wait for his next book to figure out what was happening? At times I wasn't as patient. There were days when I sat next to the telephone, hoping that the next call would be from Ariel. Marc bought me a phone with an answering system so I could have peace while being away from home.

I worked only part-time then. The children didn't have to be driven to schools anymore. Joe and Jean took a bus to their high school and Maria and Andrew walked to the recently constructed school in our neighbourhood. My Pathology class was at night. I had a new used car that looked much better than any other I had owned before.

Hanna and my other good friends were all waiting for my call from Ariel. Val and Sue gave me The Last Waltz in Santiago for my birthday. Ray phoned to wish me a Happy Birthday and asked how things were. I told him about the radio interview and Ariel's books. His reaction surprised me. He literally said to me that he had lost all respect for me because I believed that some interviewed writer was my beloved. I recited the poem about our encounter. He got even more furious. Then he asked whether the author sent me a bouquet of flowers for my birthday or phoned me from the airport. I realized that I couldn't share my joy with Ray. He was on a different plane of consciousness, fighting for his life.

The days were adding up. I began to doubt that Ariel got any message from me, nor received my cassette letter. I turned to the pages of his books and received comfort there. Manuel loved Pamela! In the book Mascara, Oriana became an obsession for the narrator. She was so different from the rest of the world that she had to be protected. Pages and pages were speaking to me. The masques that introduced themselves to me on the night of June 21st of 1989 indicated the title of this book!

When I was about to finish the course, I took on another job. I was hired as a masseuse in a chiropractor's office and had to look for my own clientele to earn money. It worked out pretty well. I worked seven days a week. Not all hours were filled with work. On Saturday nights I became a waitress again. I had to fill my time to make waiting easier. I wondered how many more hours, days, or weeks I had to wait.

In October I phoned Ariel's secretary again. She said that the tape was passed to him when it arrived. Why wasn't I hearing from him? His secretary claimed that he was an extremely busy man. How much time does a short note take? Something was happening that I didn't understand. There is no script without communication. One of my lines was missing. I had to create a change that would trigger progress, give me some incentive and inspire me to the next step. I hoped that the upcoming Christmas would bring the newness and help me to transform the present situation.

I wrapped a special gift for Ariel and placed it under our Christmas tree. It was a custom made pendant of Chilean copper that I wore at the time of our encounter. Eduardo's sister gave it to me years ago and she had engraved my name on it. The heart shaped leaf was a symbol of a leaf from our Tree of Life. Copper is the metal of Venus, the Goddess of Love.

I sent off all Christmas mail and chose a special card for Ariel, hoping that the card and the words would create a response. Yet, I was peaceful and patient. Time didn't matter. Time is linear. The quality of time mattered. I quit my part-time job and engaged in my profession only. I had Christmas holidays reserved for my family and friends. My heart was celebrating the union of Adam and Eve. I sang the sacred music daily. I sang in celebration of Melchizedek's son.

EDEN

THE winter was tough. As a matter of fact, there were days when our cars froze up and we had to wait for minus twenty degrees to get them started. On those days I had to skip work. It didn't harm anyone - clients would have cancelled anyway. I had time to study and relax a bit.

Ray was in and out of the hospital. He was on oxygen all the time. He was thin and had little energy left. Information came my way about Hydrazine Sulfate that would stop the cancer growth, but I couldn't obtain it anywhere. Antineoplastons were costly and he would have to travel to obtain them. I heard about the success of Russian physicians with their research on urine therapy. Terminal cancer patients were recovering. Ray felt reluctant about drinking of his own fountain. He still believed in a miracle cure and hoped to have more time granted to make some spiritual breakthrough.

In my colon therapy course, ozone therapy was mentioned along with its beneficial effects in the treatment of cancer and many other diseases. I had to do something quickly to keep Ray among the living a bit longer. A sudden strong impulse suggested that I should start my own clinic of alternative therapies. The health care system was in debt and we had to help to reduce it by taking good care of ourselves. I knew that in a right moment I'd be shown a clinic location and get started. At this point, I had no money for its inception, but my credit cards represented some cash. I was preparing, studying, practising. All clients I had at this time would follow me and they would refer their friends. I ordered the best massage table on the market and at the end of February I felt strongly that a certain location in the northwest of Calgary was available for me. I drove through. I found one place, but the realtor had a more affordable one coming up soon. He gave me the address. It was a place I always liked for its exposure to the public and traffic! For years, as I had been driving by, I said to myself that one day, when I'd have my own business, I would like to lease a space in that building. Now, it was almost happening.

All dealings with the realtor and the landlord went well. I still didn't have the money I needed for numerous deposits. I committed myself to March 8th. The realtor asked why March 8th. I told him that it was the day when I'd have the money. He knew that I was a single mother and he assumed that my resources were limited. On March 7th I had the money and phoned him. When he came with the offer contract, he asked me about my magic. I told him about my three lady friends who loaned me eight thousand.

"But how could you be so sure about the day?" he asked.

"It is in my destiny; I am to have that clinic. That is why all flows."

"Teach me, show me your magic!" he implored.

"You already found it. You trusted."

He turned out to be a supportive client, and every time he came, we had a good talk and much more laughter.

The clinic location was to be available and open for business by May 1st 1993. In my mind, I had a perfect place for every object, picture, poster, and plant. It was to be a healing place in harmony with the universal heartbeat. The fig tree Ray gave me a long time ago, became the major point of attraction by the entrance - The Tree of Life at Eden. I had the name for the clinic: Eden Wholistic Clinic. And I had the snake for the tree! I had the great location; the well put together brochure, and business cards.

Excited about the project, I rushed to share the news with Ray. He was still hanging in there. On March 31st I went to see him in the hospital. It was right before Easter and I knew that the Easter lilies I brought would make him happy. He acknowledged them, but could not smell the scent. He couldn't swallow anything either. I told him about ozone therapy and that he would be my first ozone client. He just said that he was very happy for me and my clinic and that he knew that I'd do lots of good. I described the place to him and how beautiful the Tree of Life from him would look there and that it would always remind me of him. He showed a little spark in his eyes, which had no colour left in them. He asked me if I could move his legs to another position. They were thin, but extremely heavy. His spirit was leaving. I told him that I'd come back tomorrow and would bring his favourite poetry. He told me not to worry about tomorrow. At that moment I knew that he was leaving us. I sat next to him on the bed, embraced him and then I held his head against my heart, rocking him gently. It was the only connection his head and mind had ever made to any heart, his own included. I kissed his crown and gently placed his head on the pillow, softly saying "See you tomorrow, Ray...."

On the way home I cried. I reviewed his life and, I ached. How many other people have dreams that never come true? How many people are up there who do something else than they were born for, never find their purpose in life, never read their own comedy! Why? Because they are afraid of a change, of the unknown, living by earthly duty and never daring to make a move and explore their own destiny. Each of them is becoming a copy of the other. How can the world progress with repeated history and do-alike? How can we possibly return to Eden with the attitude of masses? There was no way I would succumb to that movement. I was to go ahead, trusting, feeling the guidance of the spirit. Fools Day was coming and the Fool in Tarot has the highest value. It is Zero, representing the new beginning with infinite possibilities, the continuum into eternity. A circle is the symbol for the universe without the beginning and without the end - like the snake biting on its own tail.

The next day was extremely foggy and I chose not to drive to the hospital. I phoned instead. They didn't have Ray on the list. Then another nurse answered my call. She asked what my relation to Mr.

Knight was. I told her that I was just a friend. She found my name on the file.

"Ms. Heller, Mr. Knight passed away last night."

I was silent for a while. I was not surprised. I believed he went through the transition shortly after I left. The nurse gave me the public trustee's phone number.

Ray didn't make it to April Fool's Day. Perhaps, he died on Fool's Day and the next time around he'd choose a 'white dog to guide him through life', the way it was on the Celtic deck of Tarot cards he gave me.

The public trustee had no name of his relatives. I gave him some information. No one else called about Ray. The funeral service was announced in the newspaper. When I arrived at the funeral home, there was no other car parked. I asked if it was the right hour and the right place for Ray's service. It was. Ray's corpse looked peaceful. I placed one red rose into his hands and I crossed two red roses over his chest vertically and horizontally. The knight, the crusader had his rose cross. Without love and a lady to fight for, he lost his sword.

Two other people came to his funeral service. One was a nurse who said that he was such a gentleman and a sweet man. The other one was his aging neighbour who sometimes talked with him in the laundry area in the apartment building of eighteen floors. I followed Ray's body up to the burial grounds and made sure that the red roses were put to rest with him.

It was the saddest funeral I had ever attended. It wasn't my baby Jane's, who coincidently passed away on the same day nineteen years earlier, neither my father's. Ray was lonely and he died lonely and that should never happen to anyone. He was a gentleman with the name suggesting his life direction. He just never paid attention to it.

There are many pathways leading to the Kingdom of many mansions. We each follow just one. Mine was leading me to Eden, to learn about the Tree of Life. I placed the tree of life into my clinic's logo, and encoded the chemical symbol for ozone into it. My quest became the fruit of the tree from the middle of the garden.

LAMEN

THE first month at the clinic was very busy and it kept on getting busier all the time. Clients were returning, booking more appointments and many were attracted to the regeneration program I was offering. Each and every client became my partner teacher and student; everyone was so different from the other and very special. My days were long. I worked nearly ninety hours a week. I had no day off, but I loved my work and my clients. The place was bright with daylight and the plants were in their seasonal bloom, sharing the gift of fragrance. Emotionally and mentally I danced, going with the rhythm, harmony and the flow.

Jean helped a bit at home and watched over Maria and Andrew during the summer vacation. We had no more financial stress, but I had very little time for my children. I felt guilty about it. When I got home after work, I did the clinic's laundry, cooking for the next day, research work for my clients, and touched base with the children, if they were still awake. As busy as I was, I began to miss Ariel again. Why didn't he write or phone? I phoned his editor and she asked me to send a letter for him through her, promising that she'd make sure he got it. I mailed a registered letter in August.

Eden was ready for my Adam. My friend Tamarah hung the red apples on the Tree of Life. Special items in every room were ready to welcome my other half. Where was he? When was he going to appear? Each morning when I scanned the phone messages, I hoped I'd hear his voice.

The Labour Day came. It was a warm sunny day and it became my first day off, dedicated to labour - my home was turned into an immaculate place. In the afternoon, when I washed my living room window, a neighbour offered to take my children to the nearby Nose Hill Park. Her son was a sweet child, appreciating playmates. I consented. Within minutes I felt an urge to go to the clinic and check the messages. Then I began to think that I was becoming too attached to my clinic and that I must learn to stay away from it for a day, at the least. Any attachment was unhealthy and created an emotional co-dependency. I fought my desire and won. Still, I felt that my neighbour was actually giving me a message to go to the clinic and take a break. The clinic became my sanctuary where I felt absolutely at peace and at my full power. I finished the window instead, hung the curtains and went on to the next chore. When the children returned, we all took a break and enjoyed our tea time together. Again, the impulse to go to the clinic was revived. I was hesitant. Why was this happening to me? Couldn't I be separated from Eden for one day?

In the morning I got the children off to school. It was a nice feeling to have them back in their routine and with friends they had. Jean and Joe entered grade twelve. Monica had a job in Swift Current. She wanted to stay there. She was very much in love with a local man.

I rushed to the clinic to be there before ten. I turned on my messages. As usual, many callers who left no message. One beep after the other. Then my masseuse left a message and, again, many beeps. A male voice came in, leaving the most unusual statement, addressed to me: "Bye-bye, my heart angel, keep your wings of desire. LAMEN!" And he blew me a kiss that I could hear. It was Ariel's voice! I taped the message and kept on taping it until I had many calls from him between the beeps. Hanna recognized him as well. Sue and Val, the voice experts, also identified it as Ariel's. Finally, he got my letter! The message was so precious that even if

I never heard from him again, I would accept it and look forward to the next incarnation. The word Lamen was a new word in my vocabulary. What does it mean? Could it be in Sanskrit or Hebrew? I called a friend professor from the department of classics. Lamen was not in his dictionaries. My Jewish friend Iris suggested the word Lamed, which means to learn, or the introspection. What was I to learn that was so important for the next act of my comedy? More I listened to the message, more I was sure that the word was Lamen. Not any New Age devotee or a self proclaimed spiritual leader, nor a mystical teacher knew the word. Aaron was living in the Okanagan with his family at this time. I phoned him, but he wasn't familiar with the word either. Well, I decided to follow Juan's technique and release it. It would appear again at the right time.

New clients were coming in, but no Adam. Actually, none of them was named Adam. Even Romeo walked through the door! One new acquaintance passed me a business card with the logo of a bitten apple. He felt we had something in common. We both got a taste of knowledge. He was good in quoting other people, and chose well. At times he made me laugh. He didn't inspire me much, but I learned from him the slogan "A good man is hard to find, but a hard man is good to find".

Aaron dropped by on his visit to Calgary. He liked the clinic and encouraged me to give my Adam a chance.

"He is busy right now. Be patient, Ingrid. He is on his way."

"That damn Adam!" I responded. "He takes detours to Eden!"

"You're not angry with him, are you?"

"Yes, I am. All these years I've been looking for him, and when I finally find him and wait for him in Eden, he keeps silent. He doesn't even have the guts to leave his name on the tape! He leaves me 'Lamen' instead!"

Aaron looked straight at me, smiling omnisciently. Then he placed both hands over my cheeks and said very lovingly,

"All is up to you, Ingrid! You have the power to recognize the ripe fruit, so you can hand it to him. Look, how many people come to you for help, trusting you. You are a teacher! You've created something special, you had the courage. Why?"

I finished the line for him,

"Because it is in my destiny and it is in my script. Aaron, if Ariel is not in my destiny for this lifetime, I want to go beyond. I want to pass all possible lifetimes in this incarnation. I don't want to wait forever among the unborn for some fertile couple and look for my beloved again. I want to meet him this time around before I am wrinkled and weak."

"You, Ingrid? You are regenerating before our eyes; you are looking younger each time! What is your secret?"

"You know what it is. Right around the corner is our initiation room," I said, taking Aaron by his hand to the colonic room. "I am the guardian of the threshold at the bottom level!" We both laughed.

Again, I was privileged to receive Aaron's hug. We never say good-bye. We just silently part, knowing that we will cross each other's paths again.

A few days later, my friend Tamarah phoned me all excited that Ariel's play Death and the Maiden was on in Calgary. She bought me a ticket for the first night. I was ecstatic and anxious to see it. Was he so busy with this work that he could not place me into his life at that time?

After the last client left, I wandered through the clinic, being at peace. It was a sacred place, vibrant, permeated by gorgeous music. I just wished I could show the place to Ariel. I read his creation - his books. I had nothing written for him; I was not an author. I was in healing arts, opening doorways, introducing another face of God with great faith in human being; God with laughter and humour. If God didn't have a sense of humour, He would not had created us.

I sat down at the reception desk, scanning the space around me. Goethe's words that were posted on the white wall of the hallway met my sight: "Upon Faith, Love, Hope rests man's God-favoured Religion, Art, Science. These nurture and satisfy the desire to revere, to evoke, to behold. All three are one at the beginning and at the end, even if divided in the middle."

Snow began to fall in large flakes. They reflected against the clinic's lit up sign. One by one, grounding themselves to form a white carpet. To the observer they all look alike, but in reality each of them has one identical partner in design, and both are different from all others.

I phoned the children. Most of them were already asleep. I had to drive home slowly on the slippery road covered by heavy snow, but I had a certainty of being protected. What shall I do tonight to treat myself, I thought on the way. Suddenly, it occurred to me that I never read in detail the Canto XXVI of Dante's Divine Comedy. Is there some message for me, an inspiration for the next act? I brought the copy with me from A'dam's library and later on bought the John Ciardi's translation. Why hadn't I looked into it earlier?

CANTO XXVI

WHEN everyone was in bed and I knew that I would not be disturbed, I reached for my treasured file where I kept copies of The Divine Comedy. The ritual of reading special material of meditative nature created an atmosphere that was sacred, had within itself a sound of silence opening doorways to understanding and attunement with the writer and the author behind and between the lines. I was about to read the words of my Dante, who came back as a master of letters again.

Dante leaves us in the eighth sphere of the fixed stars. Examination of Love - Adam.

The poet is questioned by John about the way he came to the Possession of Love through Beatrice's eyes, that so dazzled the poet, he lost his sight. "Because the eyes of the Lady, through this land Divine conducting thee, irradiate the power that was in Ananias' hand." Dante answered, "Unto these eyes of mine, which were the gate when she brought in the fire that burns undying, come healing at her pleasure, soon or late. The Good, to this high court all satisfying, is Alpha and Omega of the scroll. Love reads me loudly or softly."

Anxiously, I took the copy of Ciardi's translation from my bookcase to compare the text. It was almost identical! I continued reading from the book.

Poet: "By the arguments of philosophy and by authority that descends from here such Love has clearly stamped its seal upon me..."

When the poet is describing love as divine, coming from praise of God, his sight is restored. "So from my eyes, my lady's eyes, whose ray was visible from a thousand miles and more, drove every last impediment away."

Beatrice: "In that ray's Paradise the first soul from the hand of the First Power turns ever to its maker its glad eyes."

Dante meets with Adam and asks him many questions.

At this point I asked myself, "When does the man meet Adam?" I had the answer, "When he has gone full circle of existences, being no more man of Exile, but returning home to Eden, having his Sophia with him. He becomes Anthropos, the complete perfected archetypal man. His sight is restored and he becomes as God."

I remembered the lecture from many years ago to which Trevor came, where the presenter spoke of The Nag Hammadí Library. She also spoke of her vision of Anthropos, and the frequency of the New Paradise, the Eden to come, without the Tree of Knowledge of Good and Evil but with the Tree of Life from the middle of the garden. This lady was a healer whose life was an inspiration. She was driven by Divine Love and transformed her life situation with victory, yet, she was so humble. Humility comes from living the truth and from the enlightenment. Pride comes from ignorance.

Ariel emanated the light of Anthropos on the Santiago street. During those few seconds of our rapture he identified himself to me. He represented my bride-groom, my Adam, my Anthropos, my other half, my twin, my beloved in Paradise. He was my male, my complementary inner masculine; my animus. He pierced my heart with cupid's arrow so the Eros would never again die and the power of love would burn all sins and transform the imperfect each time I was rewinding the scene of our encounter, just like the broken record. As long as I did that, I was running on my own battery, regenerating. The fire of divine love is the key. Indeed, my name was well chosen for me with INRI within it!

Ariel gave me a name Oriana in his book Mascara. Or, is it just my imagination? How about the pages 80 and 81 of his book? Eighty one was Dante's favourite number. It is the second power of three. I read the second half of page 80, where Ariel speaks of his novel's character being more fortunate than Adam. He wrote, "She is as Eve. But, I shall not be Adam. I shall be God and the Serpent rolled up into one, starting the day as God and ending it as the Serpent, with the chance to begin the next day another story, a new galaxy, another Garden and another Exile, until the end of time. I can rewrite and recapture the whole of human history. We can be each of the past's lovers, each character in each novel: and it will always be my narrating her, a thousand and one times, if that is necessary."

Is there some message for me in his other works? I had to die to become the maiden. I died on that street corner in Santiago, being the maiden ready for the marriage feast.

DEATH AND THE MAIDEN

THE 24th of October of 1993 was a special day. I was going to witness the success of Ariel's play. I read the play script just a few months earlier; therefore, I was aware what the play was all about. It wasn't my favourite theme but it was an important play. I had a lot in common with my twin, but had a different view on political and social systems. I believed in the evolution of consciousness and, absolutely, in no shortcuts. People earn what they are and what they have. They unfold as a blossom, gradually, in seasons of their development. Whatever happened in some countries is the reflection of consciousness of the general population. No country can be rushed through changes without its population readiness; its lack will manifest somewhere and the evident imbalance will be the result.

I closed the clinic a bit early to prepare for the date with Ariel's creation. I wore my favourite emerald green suit with matching jewellery. The theatre was full. I had a good seat. I began to read the program containing an interview with the playwright, but was interrupted by the director's introduction to the first opening night.

The play is staged in the interior of the beach house where Pauline is setting a candle light dinner, waiting for her husband. She plays the music Ombra Mai Fu, sung by a gorgeous mezzo-soprano voice. It cut through me! It couldn't be a coincidence that the piece I sang for Ariel almost daily was placed into his play! How many more surprises was I to experience? I identified Schubert's Death and the Maiden with the motif of Death from Tristan and Isolde by Richard Wagner. Both pieces create a pull on our soul, drawing us toward death without our resistance, opening for us a doorway to the magical transition. The play finished with the concert to which all three characters went to hear the Schubert's motif again, to heal, to forgive, and to begin a new life. A well done play.

During the intermission, I could overhear people talking about the play and Ariel's other works. I went to the play alone to savour the moment. I wanted to feel rather than speak. My heart became my feeling brain. When I returned home that night, I finished reading the article and placed the program into my special file. Right then I phoned Tamarah thanking her for the ticket. She was amazed that the Ombra Mai Fu was in the play. Hanna learned about it the next day. She was thrilled and reminded me to trust the process of my quest and, perhaps, to start to pay attention to the subtleties more, rather than looking outside of myself. She emphasized that the external signs are there to confirm to me that I was taking a right direction at the right pace. Hanna was an observer of my quest for all these years and she developed capacity to see it from other angles of reality. She said that her life was enriched by being my confidante and therefore her quest was happening through mine.

Tamarah loaned me her video collection of Richard Wagner's Ring she bought in Seattle. I immersed myself in the symbolism of this great work, found meanings for Tarot imagery and soon I realized that Wagner was familiar with Cabbalah and used the knowledge in his creation. Valkyrie Brunhilde was the Knight of the Golden Stone and only Siegfried, who desired his own transformation to become a King, was able to pass through the Divine Fire surrounding her.

The Creator's plan cannot be altered. Salvation cannot be stolen, neither faked. Regardless of what we believe that we are, or have, it will perish with the first blow if it doesn't have its roots deep, and high. Nothing built on sand can survive. We are powerless against the divine plan, the very blueprint of the Universe and of its activity. We cannot pretend to be gods. We can only become gods. This takes time and work. We have to prove ourselves worthy through our living, to earn the virtues, to become incorruptible true warriors of Love and Light.

On a vibration level, like attracts like, we attract what we are, we attract what we think, we can create our own world within this one. We shall be wise, for we harvest what we sow. Mind has to be disciplined, it cannot indulge in fantasies and useless daydreaming; it must create focus in a name of progress. Thinking is a responsibility and once we learn to think well, according to the Divine Law, we participate in the creation of the New World. Not the one with one currency, plastic money, and a centralized government, but the world where all minds and hearts are in harmony. Essentially, we all want the same. We desire Love, Truth, Abundance. It is in the Plan since the beginning of the creation, it is ours to begin with.

The wise minds of the past have left us a legacy in their life works. I retrieved the publication Bress 103 sent to me by the Hermetic Library's curator two years earlier. The cover displayed an alchemical drawing of the Tree of Life, its roots set deeply in the planetary bodies, the branches abundant with leaves and fruit. The fruit on one side of the tree was harvested by male hands. The fruit was not ripe. The female hands on the opposite side were harvesting the ripe fruit. The tree trunk was suspended by "hand of God" The feminine side of creation is the catalyst to the harvest. Aaron told me that I had the ability to recognize the fruit's ripeness. It is the Feminine aspect in Creation that will lead us to completion - it is Opus Feminum.

ALCHEMY

IT is inevitable. We cannot live in denial and pretend. We either settle for being just creatures of creation, or we become co-creators. The quantum leap is in the area of renaissance of the body, mind and spirit. It is about healing our temple, the body to house the spirit, to liberate it from impurities and unhealthy habits that are continuously undermining its own effort to repair itself and become available to higher frequencies for its regeneration and retrieval. The gravitational pull toward the Earth's center versus quintessence neutralizing that force. To capture the breath of the cosmos and draw it into our being, to take in the Light during timeless moments, to make our cells sing with joy and vibrate in the resonance with the Music of the Spheres. To participate in the creation of the cosmic man and woman in the image of God is the major reason for human existence and incarnations. The corporal regeneration is the prerequisite for the Great Work of the alchemist who understands responsibility with his/her own evolution. Alchemy, or the art of transmutation, involves all aspects of the human being. It is done at the physical level by means of proper body care, which may include wholistic fitness, martial arts, yoga and dance. The wholistic healing includes healthy and positive attitude toward one self and the world; it includes awareness about the process itself in order to move into the state of wholeness without discouraging obstacles. We need to re-create the harmony at the psychological level as well, and to consider our sexuality as an essential participant in the process. The external activities are always reflected internally, and vice versa. The inner work of both complementary powers of inner male and inner female polarities, represented in the symbol of medical science as two serpents of the caduceus, must be balanced. Generally, the magnetic feminine aspect is ahead of the masculine one. The balancing of both polarities within us is benefiting the nervous plexi and the health of endocrine system, which is an essential part of the solar body. Humans are multi-dimensional beings with a potential beyond their imagination. The power is released gradually into our bodies, according to the readiness and openness. At this level, there is no misuse of power; there is a constant pulse requiring steadfastness and receptiveness of the subject.

I was on my journey. I began to prepare. I wanted to be ready and didn't want to miss my, to me unknown, deadline. I added another therapy to my clinic - medical ozone, to assist people in healing, cleansing, building, and regenerating. I had the best generator and wonderful coaches. They were also very spiritual people, very much involved in higher knowledge of medicine, nature's laws and alchemy. I learned about the western alchemy and its applications. I knew for certain that by accelerating the evolution of the matter, we accelerate the evolution of the spirit. The human being is responsible for this evolution. God has done His job on our plane of existence by placing us here. We are gods now and we have to do our own healing. Healing happens when we fuse with timeless dimension of the universal consciousness where abundance on every level exists. It is like a rewinding of our present incarnation to our childhood, to the womb, when we totally merge with all creative forces of the Universe. We have to go through that gate and experience the healing crisis first. The planet has to go through the same. It is inevitable. Prophecies in The Bible actually warn us about the healing crisis. Humanity has to experience and face the accumulation of its own deeds of collective unconscious. Some spiritually developed individuals have taken on themselves some of the planetary karma, the humanity's 'sins'. Jesus Christ was such an individual and there were others in the history of mankind. They have capacity to transform and neutralize the karma of humanity. There are some of these individuals living among us today, at times in the darkest places of the largest cities, where they are needed the most. They qualified for this service; they had volunteered out of Love to do this work because it has become their next step in evolution of their own consciousness. Everyone qualifies for their own mission. None of us is free unless all of us are free. With freedom there is responsibility.

My children were still young. Joe and Jean were graduating from high school and choosing their careers. Jean was accepted in zoology study at the university, with the hope to continue in veterinary medicine. Joe was interested in mechanics. Monica went on to her favourite work and study of computer graphics. Maria and Andrew saw me a bit more because I decided to work fewer hours and take better care of myself. I worked only six days a week and continued loving every moment of it. I was a happy woman, a dancer in the Dance of Creation, swayed by its rhythm and harmonies, enjoying the leading and the strength of my partner - my Soul. I was alive! I was grateful! I was in love!

A friend, who had an interest in alchemy, brought me a book by Dione Fortune on The Mystical Cabbalah. I opened the book at the exact page where the word LAMEN was explained! I read about the Holy Grail, Alpha and Omega, Rose Cross, and the Breast Plate. I read about balance, about our personal inner work, if we ever are to become triumphant. No one can do this work for us. This work we do alone, working on our virtues. Tamino in Magic Flute did his work and could not include Pamina in it, even though she was a catalyst. We must not forget that Tamino already defeated the dragon! Pamina had to do her own work and, later on, when they were united to pass the test of water and fire, they triumphed.

The thought of the pelican landing on the balancing beam and meeting me on the other side of it filled my mind. He was the alchemical bird! Alchemists use the term pelican for one of their glass tubes used during the process of making spagyrics.

I knew my direction. The sooner I'd complete my work, the sooner I'd incarnate higher love and would meet my match. I found a meaningful message daily in the Calendar of Spiritual Truth that I had on the clinic's reception counter. The words of wisdom were provided by a lady named Mary Hayes-Grieco. One of my favourite ones said: "Healing your body, your emotions, and your mind, so that the Spirit can shine through you, is the hardest work to undertake - but, what else do you have to do?"

"He, who loves the world as his body, may be entrusted with the empire." - Lao-tzu

MESSAGES

ONE of the most satisfying human realizations is the awareness of being part of the whole. We are connected; none of us is alone. If one does something new and breaks the paradigm, someone somewhere will do it also. If one is to cut the edges, there will be a supportive body of friends who will assist in some way to reach that goal. I witnessed it in many life situations, in solidarity, in healing, in sports, in thinking and introducing new ideas and inventions. There is a constant activity; all vibrates and contracts at all times. It is like breathing. I knew well that my next step will be indicated to me. There was not much happening on the outer level, except that I'd been meeting new people, making new friends and getting better in my profession. There was a great deal of inner activity I was aware of. My dreams were informing me that all was moving in the right direction.

Tamarah left for three months to Lahore and other cities in Pakistan. She bought a silk wardrobe of many beautiful colours to match her aura and to blend with the crowd. My friend Iris went to Israel to visit with her mother and to plan a possible future move to Tel-Aviv. I thought of moving to Chile, but when? I had a clinic to operate, deeply set roots in Alberta, many friends, and my children still needed me.

Monica phoned me after Christmas from Big White in the Okanagan, where she was skiing with her boyfriend. She was getting engaged to get married. I was very happy for her and when I asked about the date, she said May 21st of '95. We were at the end of 1994. She promised that no more than one hundred guests would be invited. My parents got married on the same day fifty one years earlier.

Iris returned from Israel in the beginning of January. We spent more quality time together and I assisted her in the detoxification her body needed urgently. We always had a very special rapport together. We just flowed and laughed a lot. It was a very healing relationship for both of us. One evening, when I was done with my clients, I placed Iris in the steam cabinet while going through exciting written material on the Hebrew alphabet provided by Meru Foundation. All of a sudden, Iris asked me to get her out of the cabinet, that she had to cool fast because some special energy was coming through her and she felt it was a message for me. I assisted her and provided her own space she needed. She sat down at my reception desk and began to write something in Hebrew. I thought she wrote down her ideas. She finished one page, then looked at me, asking,

"When are you going to Chile?"

I knew that something special was happening. Never before has Iris done an automatic writing. She was aware how much I was against such practice.

"Iris," I asked, "what did you write?"

"Ingrid, this is my first time ever. It came in Hebrew! I couldn't write it in English!"

"Well, what is it? What did you write?"

Iris sat back, took a deep breath and explained,

"Hebrew is structured differently than English, but I'll do my best. Sit here next to me and write it down."

Was I ever anxious! Before I was allowed to write the first word, she said it was about me and Ariel. She said I was to write a book about us and use his real name in the book. Mystery embraced me again. I was beginning to write a very important message: "Know how to organize your affairs, put many roots down, and then tell the story right from the beginning as it happened. We are coming close to the "End of Times" and you must tell the story before then as many times as you can and write about it. Acknowledge where you are coming from, by receiving and accepting what is already here. Be open and remain open to another world and be aware about what is going on."

I was speechless for a while. I thanked the source that worked through Iris. I told her that I would call the book "The Divine Comedy by Beatrice". She loved the title.

I had no more excuses. So many times I had an impulse to begin to write about my experience, frequently being encouraged by friends. I felt very strongly that one day I would have to find the time and do it, but in what form? Iris suggested a screen play, because that way I could reach the most of population. I had no idea how much work there was involved in writing a movie script. My heart wanted to write, but at that point I had no word processor, nor the time to get at it.

The following week my friend Gaetano came to have a massage. He was all perky and excited. I thought he would relax during the massage, but his creative spirit kept on telling me that I had to write the story about Ariel and me and get at it soon.

"The world is waiting for it, Ingrid! It is a very important story! Do you realize how blessed you are to have this treasure of personal experience? All writers are just dreaming about something so true and deep. Look at them! They just write fictions! Ingrid, promise me that you will write it. You must write it!"

"Gaetano, you are my second messenger. Iris wrote a message for me in Hebrew. It said that I must write the story as it happened from the beginning."

"Exactly! Don't hold anything back. Tell it all!"

"Gae, I can only write some things, but the most important events will be there. I actually have a title: The Divine Comedy by Beatrice."

Gaetano loved the title! He began to recite to me in Italian from Dante's Divine Comedy the exact part from the Canto XXV. He was a cultured Roman, immersed totally in the Canadian life now. Gae was a writer himself, waiting for his muse, for his Beatrice.

A day or two later, one of my younger clients came for his massage. He changed his hairstyle and had a beard. When I entered the massage room, I complimented on his new look. He said that he changed his image to get into a new profession much faster. He was an assistant movie director, and he was always very busy. I was surprised that he would be willing to give up the work that he loved so much. He explained that he would like to become a producer instead. I asked my client how difficult it was to become a producer. He replied that the hardest thing is to find a good movie script the investors would appreciate. A good script was the key.

Was this a message to write a script instead of a novel? For a moment I was hesitant to say anything, but then I collected courage and told my client that I would have a very good script within two years. He felt it was a long time to wait.

"What would your script be about?"

"A true story. It is a bit mystical in nature. I would call it an esoteric thriller or a spiritual suspense."

He didn't respond, but brought me a sample of movie script. I realized how much work there was ahead of me. That same evening, when I got home, I found a computer on our dining table. I asked Jean what it was all about. She said that her father gave it to her. I asked her to teach me how to use the word processor. She vaguely agreed and warned me about the age of the computer.

"The age doesn't matter, Jean! As long as it is functional!"

She gave me a funny look. That girl had my mind!

One of my clients was familiar with all computer systems and taught me how to use it. That same evening I began to write. It took me quite a while to get used to a screen play version. I had to consider everyone involved in production, such as actors, director, camera man, producer, lighting, budgeting, name it - it could give me a split personality. I realized what a hard work it was, but I wanted to give it a try anyway.

Some friends proof read it and they loved the work. I was rushing to get ahead with it, so I could approach a professional screen writer for a feedback. Every evening I had something to look forward to. I spent hours in front of that old computer, until its sound and smell got to me. I took a three-month break.

A wonderful opportunity came my way. Through the membership in Canadian Galleries, I could take a round trip to Amsterdam, hotel and breakfast included, for nine days for only nine hundred and ninety dollars Canadian, based on double occupancy. One lady friend, who had never been to Europe and was fascinated by my reports on the Hermetic Library, wanted to come along. We travelled at the end of February, missing a terribly cold spell in Calgary.

It was so wonderful to see everyone at the Library, meet with Herman, Jacob's family, pay a visit to Nico and Key in Antwerp and connect with friends in Paris. Jan lived outside Antwerp at this time. My friend was ecstatic about it all and sometimes overwhelmed. Interestingly, in the Library she chose writings that related to her spiritual growth of that time. We photocopied pages of great manuscripts!

There was an interesting guest – a first timer. He looked for specific information on the Music of the Spheres. He had a composer friend who desperately wanted to use the harmonics in his composition. I told this young man that Genesis of the Hebrew Bible could be musically transcribed. The Music of the Spheres was encoded right there. The keys to the creative power are within the keys of musical octaves.

At this time the Library was in the hands of Dutch government. I heard that the Ster Company had financial problems, due to air travel decline, and the borrowed money from ING bank to finance the operation was due. Two years later, the Library was for sale. Based on the pressure from lobbyists, the Dutch government purchased the Library and Mr. Ritman continued in his noble work, collecting, transcribing and publishing precious manuscripts, to preserve the higher knowledge for future generations. On our last day, Herman, my friend and I were fortunate to run into Mr. Ritman on our way out. I introduced myself, thanked him for his service to humanity and asked what kind of help he would appreciate the most. He just said "Books, I need books!"

"By nature, men are nearly alike, by practice they get to be wide apart." - Confucius

The message from Iris in Hebrew (first part).

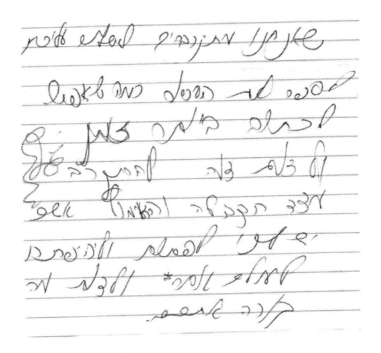

The message from Iris in Hebrew (the second part).

PENTAGRAM

MONICA was the most beautiful bride I had seen for a long time. She carried herself gracefully and was a gift to her very handsome husband. Maria was the flower girl, Andrew was the ring boy. Jean was the bridesmaid and Joe lit up candles during the ceremony.

Monica represented another Canadian home base for my children. I had only three children left to take care off. Joe was pretty independent by now. Jean was so far surviving on summer earnings and scholarships. She was an honour student.

Upon my arrival at the clinic, right after the long wedding weekend, I noticed that my clepia plant was blooming for the first time. She had a cluster of eighteen four inch long stems ending with a five pointed star of a pink colour, having a waxy appearance. They are very special plants, doing well near eastern or southern windows. Monica phoned me from the airport. The newlyweds were going for their honeymoon to Hawaii. She and her husband visited us on the way back and they both witnessed the beautiful blossoms, which dried completely three days later.

Business slowed down at the clinic. I didn't quite know how to read it, or explain it. It was unusual. I had time to write, to connect to some people after a long pause, and to contemplate. Suddenly, I began to miss Chile so much that tears filled my eyes and my body was in the anguish of nostalgia. What is this all about? Two days later one of my clients called me with very important information regarding the sale of the building where my clinic was located. This triggered the change. I was sitting at my desk and before me opened a scene of my immediate future. I was to sell the clinic and move to Chile. When? Next year.

I had something to plan for again. There was no way I could be bored with my life, or anyone who was sharing my journey. It was always exciting. I phoned Eduardo and told him about my plan. He was pleased and didn't object to the idea. He would be going home. We had a joint custody and none of us could take the children out of the province or into another country without the other party's consent. I announced my plans to a few friends and when they asked about the sale of the clinic, I told them that it would be indicated to me somehow when to start to advertise.

Iris left at the end of June for Israel. She was nervous about it. She burned all bridges, just like I did years ago, when I moved to Chile. She knew from me how powerful these moves are and how to use the opportunity for personal and spiritual growth. Iris hoped to find her beloved among her people.

I hadn't received any communication from Ariel yet, neither on our seventh anniversary. Now I had the understanding of 'lamen' and the situation. Instead of hearing from Ariel, I received three marriage proposals from three friends, to which I said "No" because I was leaving the country. Before contemplating any marriage, or a serious relationship, I had to complete what I was already involved in. I needed to go to Chile with another hundred percent commitment. I had to go back to the point of seeing Ariel last or first, to connect again with the energy that would magnify at the location of the experience itself. In Ariel's poem Vocabulary he writes: "When two of them met far away on unfamiliar street corner, they could not know if it was a first meeting, or a farewell..." I was going to go to that street corner of Ahumada and Huérfanos, feel the pavement under my soles, rewind the tape, but never rewrite the script.

At the end of July, a friend was getting married to a very nice gentleman. She was on her path full of good intentions and truly deserved the security that came with this relationship. I went to witness the ceremony in the morning and, in the afternoon I went to the clinic for booked appointments. The clepia plant was in the full bloom again! The same blossom, which was completely dried, resurrected into twenty-one star stems. Is this plant's spirit trying to tell me something? Does it bloom on wedding days?

I checked with a horticulturist to learn about the pattern of this plant. As all plants, it blooms when it is mature and the water and light conditions are right. It is the only plant he knew that resurrects its blossoms from the dead ones and keeps on adding the number of stems. This time, the blossoms began to dry on the fourth day. The fragrant pentagrams blooming in the season of their passing through the cycles of death and rebirth, in the wheel of life.

CLOSURE

SINCE it was my last year in Calgary, I had to catch up. Due to long working hours, I hadn't sung neither danced. I joined the choir to sing my favourite Bach, B-minor Mass in the spring and took dance classes for the entire year, to refresh the memory and keep up with routines.

I tried to see my older children more. Joe lived with his pretty girlfriend and Jean shared an apartment with her boyfriend, who was also a student. Monica was studying in Edmonton, driving every second weekend to Swift Current to be with her husband. Hanna and I phoned each other less. We were slowly drifting apart. I didn't expect every friend of mine to tune in. I lived too quickly, in reality I was experiencing several lifetimes in one incarnation. I knew that some relationships could not be taken into my future.

Winter was very cold and long - just another good reason to leave. I longed for longer summer season than the four months Calgary provided. We were an indoor society and it showed in the public health, facing health related issues.

The clepia bloomed in September again, but not once since then. The first week of March she bloomed in several clusters. That day I opened the Yellow Pages and looked up the business broker. The first intuitive choice is the best choice. I phoned him and he was interested. He was an intelligent man, who understood the value of my services and was eager to sell it. We had a number of interested buyers from the first day of advertisement. They all had medical background, but none of them could grasp the wholistic approach. In May, he brought a more qualified person who was a buyer. She wanted it badly and she got it. It was time to release my baby to other care giver. It was sold on the first of September.

A very dear friend was returning from Macedonia to Yellowknife and transferred in Calgary. She, her husband, baby daughter, and I met at the airport. They brought me a gift - a red Macedonian wine that was called "I Miss the South". It was named after a poem written by an exiled Macedonian poet while in Moscow. The label with the poem was attached to the bottle. I also missed the south.

Over the summer, I had to complete some unfinished affairs and work further on my book. I was writing a novel, after all. It was essential to preserve the philosophical value, which would be lost in the movie. The novel became my new project and my new baby.

SANTIAGO

THERE could not have been better timing for our trip. Canada and Chile were preparing for the Free Trade Agreement and for the first time ever, the Canada EXPO was to be held in Santiago in the beginning of December. I registered on behalf of alternative medicine and was preparing for the right representation. I needed to prepare some promotional material in Spanish and English and possibly in French. I had another reason to go to Chile! I had a furnished apartment available to rent in the heart of Santiago near the Catholic University and the General Hospital. This way, I had an address with a phone number and could have started to present my activity correctly. I certainly intended to continue my work in Chile, network in the area of alternative therapies, introducing seminars, and organize my life so my children and I could have a balanced life together.

The month of September was dedicated to clearing my household, organizing temporary storage for my books, photo albums, correspondence, which was reduced in volume with each move, and many sentimental items accumulated over the years. Amongst the stored items were two wine bottles. One was the Macedonian "I Miss the South", and the other a Bulgarian Sophia year 1988, reserved for a very special occasion. Everything else was given away to my children or friends. There was no return into any security. Our plane tickets had a return flight for the next Christmas, to visit with the other children. I was leaving behind a dozen boxes that I stored in Tamarah's house. Suitcases were packed for the most part for several months now.

In October I took the children to the west coast and Victoria. We stayed in motels and with friends in Langley. Victoria kept us well entertained for two days. We left just before the typhoon hit the island and the coast.

The drive through the Rockies was breathtaking. So much beauty is revealed, that in few hours the mind cannot keep up. A human being has the capacity to take in little by little, step by step. That way the emotional response has the potential to escalate toward ecstasy, otherwise, the experience may be too overwhelming and perceived as surreal, or as a dream. Looking at those gorgeous mountains that I never climbed because there was no man to share it with, no one who could talk to me with his eyes and feelings in perfect serenity amidst the sacredness of nature herself, I asked myself a question: Will I ever be able to share them with Ariel? Or, will there be another 'Ariel', the one who is to be my partner and consort in life? Do I really understand the mystery of the 'twin souls'? Do we grow next to the one who is like us and has the same blueprint? Climbing the third mountain is an exciting proposition, but, what if there is a cliff instead of a peak and the view of another valley and another plain opens before us? Winston Churchill once said: "It is a mistake to look too far ahead. Only one link in the chain of destiny can be handled at a time." I decided to follow his advice. Living in the present was always the secret to the mastery of life; why should I worry about what the next step will be? NOW is the most important moment in our Journey. There is its beginning and its end.

I had a few days left before our flight, for the clearing of my unresolved past and to take an inventory of all relationships, some of which would not survive the change. I was ready and open to living.

I was to leave these mountains behind, the snowy hills I skied on with so much enjoyment and feeling of freedom, one of the most magical places on the planet. There was before me another stage, a new world and continent.

On the flight from Los Angeles to Santiago, I had more time to relax and think. Maria was sitting next to me by the window. Andrew was sitting next to Eduardo right behind us. The Chilean airline service was excellent. Surrendering to the feeling of contentment, I was slowly sipping the Chilean wine, swivelling its flavour around the walls of my sensuous palate and tongue, tasting again the land of my beloved, the land that was a catalyst for my comedy; the land of fishermen, huasos, artisans, musicians, writers and poets. It is the land that trembles with earthquakes, where volcanoes erupt, where the sun rays crack the fields and the rains wash down the hills. I was to embrace that land and make it my own. It was Maria's birthplace and Andrew's cradle in my womb. In this land I'd connect to him who was my inspiration - my Dante.

COINCIDENCES

SANTIAGO had gone through a transformation since my last visit in 1988. On my way to the very core of downtown to exchange some cash, I couldn't help noticing a number of new international banks and fewer small shops. My apartment was within walking distance of the center. I took the Alameda and after passing by the hotel Libertador, I turned the corner to walk the Ahumada passage. I headed toward the street Huérfanos and to the exact place where I met Ariel the first and the last time. This time I looked at the street number. To my amazement, it was 339 and less than a meter away, on the wall leading into the passage connecting shops into the courtyard, at ninety degree angle was the number 341 - number eight in total. Right there, between the two numbers, the image of Dante stood guard at the Iannua Coeli more than eight years ago. For a while I sat on the nearby bench and observed the location where Heavens descended to Earth and souls rejoiced in praise of Paradise. While dreaming, hundreds of pedestrians passed by quickly, minding their own business and rushing to their destination. Mine was right in the center of my heart within the heart of this city, where my comedy might resume, where I would add more pages to my novel; recall the original script and act out the sacred contracts assigned to me. Fortunate I was to move with the flow of gradually released signs on the roadside of my Path! I reviewed the encounter in my memory, wondering if the law of return would manifest for me. The key players in our lives appear where they left us last. If it is not the exact place, it will be a similar location in physicality or representation. I rose from the bench, feeling slightly uncomfortable in company of a stranger who joined me and disturbed my ambience.

The center of the city was like a beehive without a queen. Now a democratic government ruled. No more organized demonstrations, no tear gas shells, no arrests. Chileans received what they asked for and what they deserved. The 1989 democratic election results surprised the world, with fifty one percent of voters deciding for the Christian Democrats and forty nine percent not wanting any change. Pinochet lost by two percent. Nobody on the street looked any happier now. In the evening, while watching the news on television, I discovered that Chile celebrated Halloween now. Chile was integrating the westernization and commercialization; it had to keep the pace with western consumerism to make banks richer. That disturbed me. I was hoping that Maria and Andrew would benefit from the way of life I remembered Chilean people enjoyed in the eighties.

Maria and Andrew were getting to know their cousins now, staying at their aunt's place in a nice district that we'd known from the past. Eduardo hoped that the immersion in Spanish would prepare them for the next school year. I was happy to have both children for some weekends or weekdays with me, but I wasn't noticing much progress with their Spanish. It turned out that they had been teaching their cousins English instead and Eduardo slacked. The immersion in the swimming pool the family enjoyed in the yard could not make up for the lost opportunity to learn the language. Though I was renting a furnished three-bedroom apartment, the children didn't like staying downtown with me much; the pollution in this hot season could be cut with knife, and the Hospital Medical Emergency Services right across the street guaranteed intolerable noise pollution day and night. We could hardly sleep; it almost drove me to desperation on some days. Writing the book took me into another world and I could cope. I also connected to people I had known in the past.

Octavio was a mature gentleman that a mutual friend wanted me to meet. His serious allergies prevented him from meeting me closer to downtown, so I ventured by bus to his place. Before I figured out that buses do not always stop by the sidewalk, but remain waiting in a middle of a busy traffic for passengers to board them, I missed a few that would take me closer to Octavio's place. Then I managed to board one, but neglected to remind the driver about my further connection. Eventually, I made it to the right intersection, realizing that I was already an hour late for my visit. I asked in a nearby restaurant about my transfer. The lady owner showed me a large map in her office and instructed me correctly how to get to Octavio's address. She was very disappointed when I told her that I would cancel today's visit, being late, and would rather phone to apologize and ask for another time. She began to insist that my friend was waiting for me and that it was important to show up, though late. Her energy was so persuasive, that I decided to respect it. She made sure that I boarded the right bus across the street. Octavio was happy that I found his place, but having plans for the evening, he invited me to join him, after we had tea and pastries.

"A friend of mine, a professor, is launching his book tonight. Would you care joining me, Ingrid? You should meet each other!"

This was very exciting. A writer, professor, his friend, me arriving late so I could share in the evening, the persuasive lady, and all this happening just one week after my arrival to Chile!

"What is the book about?" I was burning with curiosity.

"An academic material, a subject he teaches about the ethics of work. We used to be classmates – I must give him support."

I love mysteries! I wouldn't dare to ask his name, but I doubted that Ariel would lecture on the subject. We took the bus to Providencia. Octavio coped with pollution in the green belt of Santiago.

The presentation was a bit boring, but any kind of good Spanish was welcome and worthy of my time. When it was over, I was introduced to Marco and his fiery eyes. We were invited to Patio Azul Restaurant. The moment we walked in, we all headed toward a massive round table made of oak. The medieval style of interior with dimmed light was quite enchanting and it took no more than a minute and we all began to talk about the past incarnation when we could have been the "knights of the round table", while ordering our wine and meal. Marco went right to the core of our selected pleasant course of conversation.

"Did it ever happen to you that you met someone who took your breath away and you believed it was a past life connection?"

Both Octavio and I said "yes" and listened to Marco's story from his past. Octavio contributed with his fascinating story.

"I never stopped regretting my choice," Octavio admitted sadly. "I wonder what my life would be like if I had asked that lady for a date."

"Why didn't you?" asked Marco.

"I was already engaged. You know that I married very young!" he reminded his friend.

Both gentlemen met their 'special ladies' in places other than their residence and lived with regret because they didn't insist on keeping in touch. Then both looked at me and Marco asked about my story.

"And where did you meet that 'special person', Ingrid?"

"Right here in Santiago!"

As if their voices were rehearsed, both said at the same time,

"Nothing special like that happens in Santiago!"

"It did to me, during my visit here in 1988, when I walked with a lady friend on Ahumada."

Luckily our order of salad took a while and we had time to share in the story. To make it more special, we toasted with great Chilean wine and I described the encounter of the July 13th, excluding the spiritual context. They both listened with deep interest and not once would interrupt me. When I completed my tale, Octavio said that I made a mistake walking away.

Marco immediately asked,

"Any idea who is he?"

"Yes! His name is Ariel Dorfman," I answered calmly.

"I know him!" exclaimed Marco.

"I believe you," I said with an even more notable calm, almost as if it didn't matter. That surprised Marco.

"Does he know who you are? Have you met?" He was anxious to hear my answer.

"Yes, he knows who I am. I doubt he knows I'm here now."

From the beginning, Octavio suspected that my Chilean residence had other motif than taking time to write a book. In this moment he felt that he was instrumental in my reconnection to Ariel. We toasted to our comradeship again.

"Ingrid, I don't think that Ariel lives in Santiago anymore," concluded Marco.

"You are right. His parents moved to Buenos Aires and he lives in Durham, North Carolina," I explained.

"Why have you come here, then? Why don't you visit him in the United States?" Marco couldn't comprehend my logics.

"He is not just any other mysterious person. We had quite a special encounter. Deliberately I omitted the essence of it in my description to you. Sorry, gentlemen! He is a major player in my personal divine comedy. I must make sure that the sequel is not rushed or spoiled. It is time sensitive, because it opens other doors."

I really appreciated their keen perception, so rare for men of that age and intellectuality. They both had doctorate in their profession, now near the retirement years.

"I know his best friend - Antonio Skarmeta; you know of him?" asked Marco.

"Of course! 'Il Postino', the story about Pablo Neruda."

"Maybe contacting Antonio would help."

"Do you know where he lives?"

"Vitacura – he is in the phone book. Contact him!" Marco suggested.

I felt comfortable about taking that route, without breaking any rule of spiritual ethics and, I promised Marco to follow on his suggestion, thanking him.

"There are no coincidences, are there!" he collaborated.

We had a very pleasant evening together and agreed to meet again. Octavio had to return to Miami in few weeks, but Marco and I had more meaningful follow up meetings since then.

The next day, I took a bus to the residence address of Antonio Skarmeta I found in the phone book. I had a very good reason to speak with him. I brought Ariel's books along, planning on asking Antonio to obtain the author's inscription for me. The street was quiet, clean and pleasant. I rang the bell mounted on the high wall that surrounded a yard with mature trees. The family's maid, wearing a white overcoat, stepped out and I specified that I wished to speak with Mr. Antonio Skarmeta. An older gentleman with a friendly smiling face opened the gate for me and asked me in.

"You likely want to speak to my son Antonio, the writer, is that right?"

"Yes, Sir!"

He offered me a seat in the living room, explaining that his son was travelling, promoting his book.

"My son doesn't live with me anymore, but visits often while in Santiago. What can I do for you?"

I introduced myself earlier, but now I pulled out the collection of poems, The Last Waltz in Santiago and asked if he could arrange Ariel's autograph for me. He was amazed that I travelled to Santiago for that and phoned his son's home, asking his spouse about Ariel's next visit. She said that he was coming in December and again in January. She offered to take care of the inscription and Don Antonio gave me his personal guarantee.

I opened the book with the intention of marking the poem Occupation Army. I bent the corner and wrote "look here 13.7.88", explaining to Don Antonio that the poem was about my encounter with Ariel. Don Antonio's face lit up!

"Are you that lady?" The old man radiated with joy. I just nodded and smiled.

"Ariel spoke about you! Make sure you leave your phone number there. You can rest assured that he will sign the book for you!"

Then he took my hand and led me into a small room.

"Here, this is my son's room the way he kept it over the years. Ariel slept here a few times when visiting with my son. He always came over when visiting Chile. Now his parents are old. Buenos Aires is a better home for them."

I looked around the room and imagined the two young men of the same idealistic mind being best friends. The view into the yard was lovely, with trees along the pathway and shrubs below the window. The garden must have been very beautiful when Don Antonio's wife lived. She passed away in recent years, he told me. Don Antonio offered to get me Ariel's present address, but I didn't encourage it at this point. Instead, I asked about his childhood and interests. Ariel was an only child, living in Chile from his adolescent years after their residence in the United States, where the family moved from Argentina when Ariel was a toddler. Ariel's family lived in the district of the present Institute of Aesthetics, affiliated with the University. He was a gifted lad, very artistic, athletic, and a true humanitarian.

I wrote my phone number and Santiago address in the poetry book and Don Antonio passed me a note with his own address and phone number, asking me to check with him in the middle of January, when his mission would be accomplished.

I phoned him that evening, thanking him for his kindness and openness and he assured me that at his age my visit was very exciting for him. All other stimulations in his present life came from reading books. Then he recommended that I visit with Don Juan at the National Library.

"It is in your neighbourhood. Go to say "hello" from his friend Antonio. He might give you a guidance regarding publishing of your book; connect you to other writers, or translators."

I took his advice to heart and visited with Don Juan. Our friendship was unique and shortly after I met another Juan, who became a very special friend, I seldom stopped by.

Right from the start, I was taking care of all the paperwork required for my residence in the country in order to obtain a work permit. Though Eduardo was my ex-husband for over ten years, we managed to have our marriage certificate actualized to speed up a bureaucratic process. Maria was both a Chilean and Canadian citizen; Andrew had a Chilean passport qualifying him for residence and citizenship in the upcoming year. Each time I went to check on my application, the officials just asked how much money I had left to live on. It took me several months to finally understand what the intention was. I was not to obtain the permit to work as long as I had some money left.

When I was getting tired of sitting at the computer, I played board games with my children and read Spanish books to them. To their disappointment, most of the Christmas gifts they received from me were books. Often we watched television - some were good programs. It helped us with Spanish, which sounded like Spanglish at this level. On one hot afternoon, after we browsed through the artisan market, I made a banana milk shake. Maria didn't care for it and Andrew took just a sip. The blender was full of the thick delight I couldn't possibly waste. I drank it all by myself. Two hours later, I started to feel queasy and that same night I had fever. Andrew told me it was from the shake. My heated up lungs could not tolerate the icy milk beverage. I came down with pneumonia. Eduardo picked the children up and I tarried in my own care, knowing what to do. Juan worried and brought me fruit sometimes. He phoned daily.

I was near recovery when I phoned Don Antonio about the autograph. He promised he'd check with his son. I was anxious. Suddenly, I had an intuitive hunch that Ariel might come to our meeting location on the six-month anniversary. I marked the date of our encounter in his poetry book in the North American way, without crossing the seven, which would look like number one – January. The night before the anniversary I was intensely thinking about this possibility and planned on showing up by the number 339 on Ahumada at three-twenty in the afternoon. Recovering from pneumonia, I needed to catch up with my writing. I lost the track of time, when I felt a blow right into my stomach, as if a fist punched me. I checked the time. It was five to three! My God, I cannot make it on time! I panicked, but calmed down quickly, accepting the reality and letting go of my premeditated idea that Ariel and I would meet for the second time. I resumed writing when another strong punch in my solar plexus alerted me. The computer clock showed twenty past three. In that instant the phone rang. I picked it up saying "Hallo!" There was silence, but I heard a street tumult in the background. I repeated my initial "hallo" and received from the caller a self-evident deeply sorrowful sigh. The succession of thick silence could not be conquered by downtown bedlam; it was like an echo of the regret I carried inside me till then. I think we both hung up the receiver at the same time. The time of maturity had not reached its season.

PRIORITIES

EDUARDO took on the responsibility of negotiating schooling for our children within the public system. Most of schools in good districts were full, but he managed to register the children in the area of Vitacura close to Las Condes. It was, according to him, the second best of public schools. I began to look for a place to rent near the school. I found a three-bedroom house within walking distance. The yard needed lots of work, but that was something I enjoyed doing. Otherwise, the house was renovated and clean. I bought a gas stove and a sofa bed that Maria used at night for bed. Andrew slept on a foam mattress and I used my massage table for sleeping. We lived on Virginia Street. Before we moved there, I wanted to show the children the countryside where we lived in the eighties and where Maria spent the first two years of her life.

We took a bus. I was eager to see the Cordillera and introduce the beauty of the sixth region to my children. What a letdown! Not even the small hill close to the highway could be seen through the thick smog. When we walked toward Graneros off the highway, I was not feeling well. My voice became hoarse, my eyes watered, I felt itchy. I reacted to the pollutants. The children disliked walking on the endless country road without a view. Our former house was abandoned now and the well was empty. We hoped to visit Pilo, but he was a hired hand on a horse ranch in the next region now.

Patricia offered to show us the way to visit him one day. Other friends in town were home and very happy to see us and meet the children. They acknowledged that I had environmental allergies and we expanded on the subject. For the last years, the agriculture had become controlled by American companies that insisted on the use of chemical pesticides and herbicides, implementing first experimentation with genetically modified seeds, destroying the livelihood of small farmers. The profits were placed ahead of nature and public health. Stillborn and deformed babies were born, the young boys of poor families who worked for farmers, fumigating fields without oxygen masks, were becoming seriously ill, and other defects began to surface. The mutation of species was enforced and Chile was condemned. I began to question my choice of living in Chile.

For some time, I had attended gatherings of English speaking foreigners whose spouses worked in Chile, mostly in professional positions. My initial contact was made through the Expo, where my booth was the busiest one, right after the beer-tasting booth. I gained two clients whose health improved tremendously due to my services. Then ladies from 'our English community' gave me a chance and booked massages for their hard working spouses as well. I was able to buy groceries and pay my bills. My savings were already used up for the rent and damage deposit payments. The cost of living in Chile was much higher than in Canada, with much smaller earnings for most. Faithfully, I attended functions organized by the Canadian Embassy, including a charitable silent art auction, where I met more people and increased my clientele. No matter how much I tried to get ahead, I began to face other obstacles. The season began to change rapidly and I could not afford any heating device. We were cold in our house and my clients booked fewer massages. Due to humidity, the sheets and towels would not dry on time either.

The children lived with me full-time since my move from downtown. The school had two classroom shifts. Maria had morning classes, Andrew the afternoon. I spent hours helping the children with homework and the language. Whenever I could, I worked in the yard. The dead lawn behind the wall surrounding the house was transformed into a fertile vegetable garden. The front yard, visible to everyone, looked so much better now with perennials I received from neighbours next door and from the Ambassador's garden. Our outdoor environment was pretty, but indoors we had an obvious lack. A Canadian friend offered to buy my ozone generators. I consented to one sale, at first. Her husband practised Chinese medicine in Rio de Janiero, while she travelled, promoting his services. He was a Master of his craft. This money helped us to catch up with bills, refill the gas bottle and purchase some food.

At the end of March, my daughter Jean called with good news from Calgary that she had been accepted into the Veterinary College in Saskatoon. This information triggered my decision to return to Canada. Andrew was concerned about our move, while Maria was open to our return. Most of their relatives lived in Chile, but three siblings lived in Canada. The decision was made. Eduardo didn't like the idea as much. My friend bought the other generator and we planned our return just two months before the anniversary of the encounter with Ariel. The future of my children mattered. My personal journey was entwined with theirs; their future and success in life was directly linked to my choices. That was the reality of the time. I was convinced that I made the right decision when I went to school for parent/teacher evening. The classroom looked like a prison cell with a bonus large window. There could not be a comparison to any classroom in Canada. I needed to rescue my children from this environment and place them where the hand of destiny directed. Returning in May, we had hope that both children could satisfactorily pass the school grade they would miss otherwise.

On nice days, we travelled to visit with friends to see them one more time, perhaps the last time. Juan came by one day, sad about me leaving. He said that I had the Chilean situation well figured out, observing the amazing growth and development to blind the investors, the prosperous working population driving leased vehicles, with non-repayable loans through credit cards, and the availability of bank loans for working poor. The repossession of estates by banks and creditors were on the rise. The country rich in resources, the country with balanced economy in the recent past, had become a prey to exploitation. "Not a good future for our children", he said. "You are lucky to have another homeland." He blessed my decision.

I had to choose dry and sunny days for packing our suitcases. My books were much heavier due to humidity in the air. Though taking less with us this time, the weight of luggage exceeded the expected limit. Many items were pre-sold to people who asked for them. I had a buyer for everything replaceable. Our flight reservations were booked for Mother's Day, just like thirteen years ago, when I was pregnant with Andrew.

I went downtown one more time to feel out the location on Ahumada and to part with Juan from the library. To my pleasant surprise, Don Antonio also waited for him.

"What a coincidence!" he exclaimed. "I was going to give Juan this note for you. Here, take it!" and he passed me a small folded paper with Ariel's home address and phone number.

"What happened with the autograph?" I asked concerned about the book that was so precious to me.

"Ariel had to leave Santiago in a hurry. His Mother was not well. My son had arranged to visit him in the United States and he is taking your book with him. I need your present address to send it to you."

"Don Antonio, I'm leaving Chile. I need to take my children back to Canada."

He looked at me with sadness, as if a nice dream left his world.

"You are coming back, are you not?"

"Not for a long time. I have responsibilities with my family."

He reciprocated with an evident empathy in his eyes. I wrote down a friend's address in Calgary. When I passed it to Don Antonio, he added,

"You know that Ariel travels to Santiago twice a year, at least!"

"I am aware of that, Don Antonio. He is a Chilean citizen - he must."

Without doubt, I was abandoning my quest through the land Ariel loved so much. I parted in a very amicable way with Don Antonio, thanking him for his contribution and wishing his son success. When almost everyone left the area, I informed Don Juan about my departure and also thanked him for his help in the past. We had a very interesting conversation after. He was one of the most well-read people of that country, knowing the world of matter, but I introduced him to the world of Spirit that he found so fascinating.

On the way home to the house on Virginia, I read the address of Ariel. There was a fax number and the phone number. I phoned the number in the evening. The number contained two "3s", one "7" and "88". The final digits of his number contained the date of our encounter! How sweet! A woman's voice answered and I asked in Spanish to speak with Ariel. She replied that he travelled a lot and that she was his tenant on Campus Avenue. She offered to pass him a message. At that point I asked her about the phone number I called. She said that he had it for years and didn't want to change it. The house was rented with the phone number. I wanted to spare the lady from any other involvement, thanking her for her kindness.

On our departure day, more people came to see us at the airport than on the day of our arrival. Eduardo was to follow us in two weeks. My massage table and five suitcases were directed to Los Angeles, where we had to pick them up for our flight to Calgary.

Comfortable in my seat, carried on the wings of the Lan Chile aircraft, I reviewed the journey and what it accomplished. Though I hadn't completed the book, I had it all in my mind, very much alive. Was my comedy over? Shall I draw the curtain and close the script? I, the three times blessed Beatrice, now between Heaven and Earth, have surrendered to my senses, swivelling and appreciating the Chilean wine, enjoying the moment. I immersed myself in the essence of the experience itself, in the ability to breathe and hear the blood rushing through the arteries; the world within, the ineffable, the infinite and absolute.

REFLECTION

THE world within and without, "as above, so below", the reflection of microcosm in the manifestation of the macrocosm, that is what Life Drama is all about. If not much is happening on the outside, likely not much is happening on the inside, unless the constant anxiety is telling us that a deep investigation of our present life situation is urgent. The human being was endowed with spirit, was assigned an individual soul, has a full-time assistance of the subconscious mind; was given the tools to garden and to harvest the fruit.

More enlightened research scientists are looking to the macrocosm to understand the microcosm. They study astronomy and relationships of galaxies, black holes, warm holes, and try to identify the unified-field of quantum physics.

Due to that approach, progress was made in microbiology, research in neurology and other fields directly related to human ecology. The Universe is an intelligent culture of civilizations governed by laws of nature that can be applied on all levels and dimensions of its manifestation. And there is mathematics, the most fascinating adventure into past, present and future, based on a precise science of logic, and also on imaginative progressive thinking processes. Answers to the understanding of life and universe, no matter how far our mind's eye can see, rest within the human being.

Greek philosophers and Jesus of Nazareth referred us to our center, the "Kingdom within"; we are made in the image of God – we are the reflection of the Creator and His Creation.

The Journey in the external Life is the mirror reflection of our inner journey. We just need to learn how to read our personal book of life, the traffic signs along its path, and to pay attention to the silent language of the spirit. Fortunate and wise are the individuals who have taken interest in the study of metaphysics, parapsychology, Cabbalah, Genesis, some parts of the Old Testament and New Testament, Revelation of the Bible and other related scriptures, in Veda teachings of Hindus, Greek mythology, sacred geometry, and who are contemplating its wisdom and guidance.

Externally, I have met my male that reflected my inner masculine side. Being a single mother for many years, I had the opportunity to strengthen those masculine qualities required for the role of both the mother and the father. I became quite independent in many ways and took responsibility in becoming the provider on many levels. I could execute tasks usually assigned to men, I was a resourceful homemaker and positively I was a mother and nurturer. I took on a feminine role in all imaginable expressions. I had within me balanced genders; I was ready to meet my other half. In all my life stages, I have been meeting the complementary opposites in the other gender. Where I lacked, they compensated, and vice versa. The life cycles have been opening their time sensitive windows of opportunities for the next step toward my completion, and make me whole.

Our spiritual development is co-dependent on the completion of the preceding assignments in our life. Before being granted a higher experience, we must complete with the former one. There is no shortcut; neither can we pretend that we have reached a certain point. The Moon, the Sun, and the Truth cannot be hidden. What we have earned on the inner levels will appear before us in the world of matter. Coincidences, synchronicities, messengers, the revealing dreams – all are indications that we are walking the talk. The voice of our Soul cannot be mistaken with any other. It simply resonates in our heart. It is the most important relationship we can ever have.

The inner Journey is the key to reach our personal Mount of Olives and enter Paradise. I am very grateful to my Soul for its guidance, showing me direction in Life and gifting me with awareness of my past, present and future. I also am very grateful to my Soul Mate for his courage and dedication, for his armour of the Spiritual Warrior, and to the playwrights of our Divine Comedy.

The Journey is on .... perpetually ascending toward a higher experience from the previous one, both meeting in the present moment of the Now, where the many doorways of possibilities await our Dream of desired Future. Which one is the right one to open and energize? That, itself, is the Gift from the Creator: it is up to us to create what we want. We have a free will at our disposal - we have the power to create. Within the Sea of Consciousness, we are recognized by our own creation. We must make sure that what we begin to manifest is truly what we can accommodate in our living existence, and that we are ready for consequences and its fruit. There is no point of return then – there is only a way ahead. Let's create wisely, then!

I know what I want! Love, Peace, Joy, Harmony, Health, Abundance and Creativity for myself and for the reflected masculine aspect of my inner Beloved in the World of Matter and, for my Sister Humanity I want the Awakening to a realization that it is our birthright to create a Dream of living in Love, Peace and Joy. Practise loving each other unconditionally – no more is expected of us. With Love we fulfill the Dream of our Creator and the Dream for His Beloved Creation.

**The Fruit of the Tree of Life is
indeed sweet and delicious in Paradise.**

ABOUT THE AUTHOR

BORN in Czechoslovakia in 1946, Ingrid Heller grew up in Liberec in Northern Bohemia, enjoying the romantic environment of her culturally and industrially developed hometown. Her interest in nature, arts and music was nurtured since her early childhood. After the Warsaw Pact army invaded her country in August 1968, she left her beloved homeland. Since 1969 she has resided in Calgary, Alberta, Canada, where she raised her five children. She shares her residence between Calgary and the Kootenays area in British Columbia. She also lived in Chile for three years with her family. Brought up and educated in an atheistic society, Ingrid looked to nature and human beings for the answers to the mysteries of life. Fascinated by both the complexity and simplicity of nature's laws and human existence in their physical and spiritual expression, she eventually became a wholistic practitioner, engaging in effective therapies and enjoying results of nature's wisdom.

Her book "The Divine Comedy by Beatrice" based on a true story was published in 2001.

"Footprints in the Andes", published in 2004, describes what her family had to endure during their residence in Chile.

"The Wise Pussy Tales", the erotic memoirs, offer the peek into metaphysics of sex.

"Betrayal of the Beloved", also based on a true story, is provoking thoughts regarding detachment, compassion and forgiveness. Published in 2009.

For retreats and seminars presented by Ingrid and the team, visit e-mail: ingridheller88@gmail.com

For deeper understanding of the Creation and its Matrix, visit www.probablefuture.com and find out how you can personally participate in the creative process on behalf of the Creator.
e-mail: odonnell@gate.net